Praise for Michelle Arnot

"One of the clearest, liveliest, and most entertaining writers in the world of puzzles."

—Will Shortz, crosswords editor of the *New York Times*

"Beginners and pros alike will enjoy Michelle Arnot's insight into the world's greatest pastime."

—Marilynn Huret, www.garfieldgames.com

"Michelle Arnot really knows the world of puzzles."

—Janis Weiner, editorial director of Kappa Puzzle Group

FOUR-LETTER WORDS

AND OTHER SECRETS OF A
CROSSWORD INSIDER

—■ ■■—

Michelle Arnot

A Perigee Book

A PERIGEE BOOK
Published by the Penguin Group
Penguin Group (USA) Inc.
375 Hudson Street, New York, New York 10014, USA

Penguin Group (Canada), 90 Eglinton Avenue East, Suite 700, Toronto, Ontario M4P 2Y3, Canada
(a division of Pearson Penguin Canada Inc.)
Penguin Books Ltd., 80 Strand, London WC2R 0RL, England
Penguin Group Ireland, 25 St. Stephen's Green, Dublin 2, Ireland (a division of Penguin Books Ltd.)
Penguin Group (Australia), 250 Camberwell Road, Camberwell, Victoria 3124, Australia
(a division of Pearson Australia Group Pty. Ltd.)
Penguin Books India Pvt. Ltd., 11 Community Centre, Panchsheel Park, New Delhi—110 017, India
Penguin Group (NZ), 67 Apollo Drive, Rosedale, North Shore 0632, New Zealand
(a division of Pearson New Zealand Ltd.)
Penguin Books (South Africa) (Pty.) Ltd., 24 Sturdee Avenue, Rosebank, Johannesburg 2196,
South Africa

Penguin Books Ltd., Registered Offices: 80 Strand, London WC2R 0RL, England

While the author has made every effort to provide accurate telephone numbers and Internet addresses at the time of publication, neither the publisher nor the author assumes any responsibility for errors, or for changes that occur after publication. Further, the publisher does not have any control over and does not assume any responsibility for author or third-party websites or their content.

First edition: August 2008

Library of Congress Cataloging-in-Publication Data

Arnot, Michelle.
    Four-letter words : and other secrets of a crossword insider / Michelle Arnot.
        p.   cm.
    "A Perigee Book."
    Includes bibliographical references.
    ISBN 978-0-399-53435-5
  1. Crossword puzzles.   2. Crossword puzzles—Anecdotes.   I. Title.
    GV1507.C7A75 2008
    793.73'2—dc22   2008014260

PRINTED IN THE UNITED STATES OF AMERICA

10   9   8   7   6   5   4   3   2   1

Most Perigee books are available at special quantity discounts for bulk purchases for sales promotions, premiums, fund-raising, or educational use. Special books, or book excerpts, can also be created to fit specific needs. For details, write: Special Markets, Penguin Group (USA) Inc., 375 Hudson Street, New York, New York 10014.

CONTENTS

A Puzzle a Day: Adventures with Crosswords vii

1. WHY FOUR-LETTER WORDS?
   The Anatomy of a Crossword 1

2. DECODING CLUES:
   How to Solve for Four-Letter Words 14

3. THE FIRST LADY OF FOUR-LETTER WORDS:
   Margaret Farrar née Petherbridge 25

4. FOUR-LETTER WORDS IN THE *NEW YORK TIMES*:
   All the Puzzles That Are Printed to Fit 36

5. KEY FOUR-LETTER WORDS STARTING WITH **E**:
   A Chain of Crossword **E**'s 51

6. AROUND THE WORLD IN FOUR-LETTER WORDS:
   Armchair Traveling 68

7. FOUR-LETTER SURNAMES:
Hello, **DALI** 88

8. FOUR-LETTER FIRST NAMES:
Who's Who in Clues 103

9. THREE-LETTER WORDS:
The Shortest Repeaters 115

10. BRITISH FOUR-LETTER WORDS:
Cryptic Crosswords 132

11. FOUR-LETTER WORDS OUTSIDE THE BOX:
Crossword Variations 144

12. FOUR-LETTER WORD DASH:
Solving Against the Clock 157

13. THE FUTURE OF FOUR-LETTER WORDS:
"The — the Limit" 172

Appendix 185
Essential Crosswordese 189
Bibliography 209
Acknowledgments 213

A PUZZLE A DAY:
Adventures with Crosswords

"You must have a great vocabulary!"

New acquaintances often exclaim this, to my embarrassment, when they learn that I've served as editor and publisher of dozens of national puzzle magazines over the past two decades. If I had a nickel for each time I have heard that remark, I'd be able to make a down payment on a Park Avenue **AERIE** (*puzzle clue:* "Penthouse"). Most people assume I am a walking dictionary due to my years as an *acrossionado*, to use a word I made up to describe my career as editor of five volumes of *Crosswords for Dummies* and many years with the Kappa Puzzle Group (over a hundred publications, including the four-color *Games* magazine, *New York Times* editor Will Shortz's old stomping ground).

The embarrassing truth is that my vocabulary is disproportionately skewed toward four-letter words. Not the naughty ones that have made themselves at home in print nowadays but the cute, oddball four-letter words that grout the grids of American crosswords. Puzzle solvers recognize that the basic lingo of the daily grid consists mainly of unspoken words, phrases, and even fragments. Due to the peculiarities of their letter structure, four-letter-type words prop up the puzzle. Getting to know as few as twenty-five of these handy words can boost one's solving abilities significantly, not to mention one's ego and brain power: four-letter words like **OGEE** (*puzzle clue:* "Curved molding") and **TSAR** (*puzzle clue:* "Ivan, for one"); the **ABBA**, **BETA**, and **FALA** vowel-heavy combinations that give those in the know a jump-start. I write the answers in all capital letters because upper-case letters are the currency of crosswords. No cursive in this world; back to grade-school letters that are legible in their little boxes.

Undoubtedly, Miss Wohl, my third-grade teacher, had no inkling how studying the crossword in my *Weekly Reader* would ultimately determine my livelihood. Even then, I tried my hand at creating puzzles for a class magazine that I co-edited with my best friend. I got some things right, like ending a word with a black square, interlocking words across and down, and checking the spelling of the words I selected. But I didn't yet understand that crossword grids have specifications and that their patterns are symmetrical.

As you'd expect from a compulsive solver, my hobby won me a spelling bee prize from *The Journal American.* Yes, I was (and continue to be) a confirmed bookworm, fascinated by the way grids weave words together in black and white. Four-letter words appeal to me. Call me a word **NERD** (*puzzle clue:* "Egghead sort"), but ever since 1977, when *New York Times* crossword editor Eugene T. Maleska paid me $20 for my first crossword, I have become fluent in crossword clichés.

■ ■ ■

I am an alumna of the Weng school of puzzle solvers, a short-lived era by crossword standards. *Weng* is the editor Will Weng, clue stylist at the *New York Times* in the 1970s. At the time, I was enrolled in a New York City high school. It didn't take long to bond with the puzzle lovers among my classmates. From that moment, I embarked on a lifelong dialogue with the puzzle-solving community. My schoolmates and I giggled or groaned over Weng's clues. "Organs often lent" (**EARS**), "First Lady's first name" (**BESS**), "Barnum's egress" (**EXIT**), and "Act of a sort" (**RIOT**) had us in stitches. Whimsical Weng reeled me in with his sly humor. How quaint my compulsion seems by contrast with the way today's teens spend down time with texting, using AOL Instant Messenger, or listening to an **IPOD** (*puzzle clue:* "Song holder")!

What a frisson when I discovered that the chairman of the

history department at my high school, E. Ira Marienhoff, contributed to the puzzle page. In the dark ages of the 1970s, twenty years before the *New York Times* introduced bylines to the crossword, I stumbled upon this juicy "Morsel" (**ORT**, as puzzle solvers call it) while absorbed in a *New York Times* crossword before class. By contrast to twenty-first-century teachers, educators during the era of **HAIR** ("1968 rock musical") kept students at arm's length. The only tidbit we had on Marienhoff was that he lived with his mom. The other publicly known fact about the man is that he left an unexpectedly significant endowment to Yeshiva University in 1994, which generated some local publicity.

Upon seeing me with the puzzle, Marienhoff revealed that he was its author. That was my lightbulb moment: A high school teacher could make up a puzzle and get it published. He told me that the editor sent out guidelines upon request and that anyone could make one up and submit it. This became the lesson from A.P. history that influenced the course of my adulthood. No telling how what you hear in the classroom may direct you down the road.

∎ ▪ ▫ ▪

Not until graduate school at Columbia University did I take the time to craft a puzzle and mail it in with a **SASE** (*puzzle clue:* "Ms. enclosure"), as publishers refer to the self-addressed stamped envelope. By then Maleska had succeeded Weng.

Maleska, a former high school administrator and a poet, had sent me guidelines with a handwritten note in which he expressed excitement that a young person was entering the field because most of his regular contributors were retirees. He worried that the field would suffer without new blood and inquired whether I had heard of a graduate student in the Midwest, a prolific puzzle constructor by the name of Will Shortz. That surname made an impression on me, as it has since on millions of crossword fans.

Mimeographed sheet in hand, I invested in the primitive tools of a constructor from the Jimmy Carter era: lead pencil, clean eraser, and a packet of graph paper. The guidelines informed me that the grid for a daily crossword measures 15 × 15 squares, of which no more than one-sixth are black. Next, I thought up a theme (the common thread that typically connects the three longest horizontal entries in the grid). I studied the various designs and adapted one that worked with my theme. Then I scribbled and erased for a week.

Later that year my submission appeared in print. It was on a Tuesday, I believe, which experienced solvers understand means it was on the easy side. (The *New York Times* crossword ramps up after Wednesday to the Saturday hair puller. Some of my closest friends don't even bother with a *New York Times* crossword before Thursday.) For my week's labor in 1977 I received a check in the amount of $20. By the time Shortz took the reins of the *Times* puzzle in 1993, daily constructors received a whopping $50. Thanks to Shortz's lobbying, as of June 2007 the price tag on a daily puzzle is now $200. Of course, today's tools of the trade—a computer and the Internet—require a much greater investment than my modest tools. For a Sunday crossword, the *Times* shells out $1,000, up from $700. On an hourly basis, that pays the Starbucks bill, although not much more in the final analysis.

A casual remark to a fellow Columbia student in September 1977 about how I had taken time off from the study of semiotics to compose a crossword led to my introduction to Professor Emeritus Eugene Sheffer. For the second time in my academic life, my most valuable lesson at school led me away from academia and deeper into the world of crosswords.

Sheffer, a bachelor who had conducted a lifelong affair with the French language, sold his first puzzle in 1920 at age fifteen for $5. Not bad, if you consider the buying power of a buck in the '20s! He conducted two parallel careers: professor and puzzle constructor for King Features Syndicate, which provides its puzzles to hundreds of newspapers around the nation. At Columbia University, he served as director of La Maison Française from 1942 until 1966, earned the Légion d'honneur, and made fast friends with four-letter *puzzle clue:* "Parisian singer Edith" (**PIAF**). Although he was diagnosed with dystonia while an undergraduate, the neurological disorder did not prevent him from earning a doctorate from the University of Grenoble in 1929 and teaching French for over four decades at Columbia University. He was just considering whether to hang up his pencil or look for a new assistant when we met. One of his earlier Columbia University assistants, Jack Kerouac, assisted on translating French textbooks and even "ventured definitions for *The Journal American* crossword," according to Kerouac's recollections in *Atop an Underwood*.

At our first meeting, Sheffer asked to see my published puzzle in the *Times*. We compared notes on what we liked as solvers, and by the end of our visit I got the job offer: Would I work with him on the King Features crosswords? Semiotics never seemed less compelling as I accepted the job, a position I retained after leaving graduate school and until the end of his life four years later.

During my apprenticeship to Sheffer, my main responsibility was to support the output of six puzzles per week, Monday through Saturday crosswords. He provided me with a series of numbered black-and-white preset patterns that repeated in sequence every six weeks. The 13 × 13 grids were smaller than the daily *New York Times* crossword. Our target solver was the commuter, either sex, with a high school diploma or higher. "Middle society" is how Sheffer described his fan base, not quite the *New York Times* crowd; and that is the group for which I have provided puzzle entertainment ever since.

Born in 1905, Sheffer was eight years older than the first crossword puzzle, which owed its existence to the *New York World*. All the tales the professor shared with me were much too juicy to keep to myself. I put them all down on paper, and eventually they made it into my book *What's Gnu?: A History of the Crossword Puzzle*, which entered bookstores a few months after my mentor passed away, leaving a hole in my life. Most puzzle solvers are familiar with the South African **GNU** (*puzzle clue:* "Antelope's cousin"); with dark horns, vertical mane, zebra head, and bovine hindquarters, it has the patched-together look of a crossword puzzle.

■ □ ■

When I was editor and publisher of the *Herald Tribune* crossword magazine group during the Reagan **ERA**, I conducted a series of interviews with celebrity *acrossionados*. Some of the chapters ahead begin with sound bites from those chats. During a memorable lunch with cartoonist Roz Chast, she confided to me that despite lots of puzzle practice, the slippery four-letter words that everyone else seems to know continued to elude her. Her biggest bugbear was *puzzle clue:* "Finnish architect Saarinen," the perennial **EERO**, whom she tried to dub **ERIC**. She also struggled with the answer for *puzzle clue:* "Asian governess," which she knew started **AMA** but debated about the last letter. It ends unpredictably for English speakers, but helpfully for puzzle constructors, with an **H** for **AMAH**. *Puzzle clue:* "MD's org." yields **AMA**, short for American Medical Association.

The first female cartoonist on contract with *The New Yorker*, Chast maintains an astonishing output, considering that she juggles work with a family and keeping up on first-run films. Predictably, my personal favorite Chast cartoon is titled "Answers to Last Week's Puzzle: A Toughie" (*The New Yorker*, June 13, 1982). She describes this piece as her "revenge" on crosswords. It depicts an answer grid that reads sensibly in all the Across words, while the Down entries are a string of nonsense words. Four bemused faces stare at the answers from both sides. The message underscores her ultimate complaint that she becomes doubly frustrated when she finds out that a Down answer like **OHPT** is a real word.

Just kidding! **OHPT** is not a valid four-letter word but a spoof on the type of words familiar to puzzle solvers who have hung out with the grid. It's meant to evoke that sinking feeling that inexperienced puzzle solvers face when they see a series of letters that make no sense to them. Puzzle constructors abide by strict rules that require what they put in the grid to appear in the dictionary or equivalent reference. If **OHPT** should emerge in a crossword in progress, the professional puzzle constructor will stop cold! In the early years, puzzle constructors stooped to the use of a biblical figure named **OHEL**, who answered *puzzle clue:* "Zerubbabel's son." But he has dropped from sight. After some erasing and testing of new letters, today's puzzle constructor would go for an acceptable four-letter term like **APPT** (*puzzle clue:* "Diary abbrev.," for a shortened version of the word *appointment*). Or, by replacing the middle two letters, the word could turn into **OMIT** (*puzzle clue:* "Leave out"). Or the puzzle constructor might just insert a full-fledged **O** repeater like **ORCA** (*puzzle clue:* "Killer whale") or **OSTE** (*puzzle clue:* "Bone: prefix"). When changing a series of letters, the puzzle constructor checks all the words that interlock to make sure that they conform to the guidelines.

Obscure words do make their way into the crossword, but they are the exception. What Chast's cartoon conveys is how puzzles invite kooky words and abbreviations to make themselves at home in the grid. They pop up time and again, and getting to know them makes the difference between finishing a puzzle and giving it up. To the untrained eye, these words may look like gobbledygook. Experienced solvers, however, have a handle on the formulaic four-letter words and their matching puzzle clues. As with any game, you need practice.

A degree in linguistics is not a prerequisite for competent crossword solving. Nor do you have to be a word nerd. To get to square one, you need a sense of humor and a writing implement. To these add a passing knowledge of the dialect that puzzle people call *Crosswordese*, the special vocabulary that makes puzzles tick. I shared these words in the curriculum of an adult education course I devised for the New School for Social Research, in New York's Greenwich Village. Like solitaire, puzzle solving is a solo pastime. You can do it your way or you can try my suggested strategy. Like the practice of yoga, there is no right or wrong way to do puzzles. What I offer is a series of steps that, in my experience, has proven to work like a charm.

How does a solver think? Tackling this question informed the way I structured the course. The idea struck after an epiphany provoked by *puzzle clue:* "WWII battle site." I was struggling with the pronunciation of the strangely spelled **STLO**, which I knew was the correct answer. What stumped me was how to say it. But who to ask? I didn't know any speakers of Crosswordese; so in that pre-Internet time, I opened my atlas. Looking at a map of France, I realized inserting a hyphen in the middle of the word turned the answer into a city in Normandy: St-Lo, or Saint Lo, the site of a three-week siege in July

1944, which became a turning point for the Allies' ultimate victory. Yes, it is humiliating to admit my sketchy knowledge of World War II battles. But the reward was a lesson in geography and history. From that episode, I recognized how puzzle solvers could benefit from a forum and from speaking the forbidden four-letter words. Folks came from every borough to take a break from their favorite solitary pastime to discuss it with others.

In the classroom, I discovered that puzzle solvers are a talkative bunch. After all, when you work on a puzzle you are left to your own thoughts. You have moments of discovery and moments of frustration. What a luxury to have a place to vent! What do people who love puzzles talk about when they talk shop? Without a rule book or instruction manual, discussion ranges from wordplay and clever clues to the challenge of grids with wide open spaces to the Sunday indulgence of the bigger crossword and to the feeling of deprivation when a day passes without a crossword.

The evening course attracted folks from a fascinating array of day jobs, most memorably one man who traveled the world as a judge for cat shows. A vocation that operates like a vacation! Cats and crosswords, two compatible passions. Puzzle solvers cut a wide swath, from actor Matt Damon to author Russell Baker to President Bill Clinton, from actress Celeste

Holm to television personality Dick Cavett to rock star Sting, who was photographed working a puzzle en route to Madonna's wedding to Guy Ritchie. Musicians are naturally adept at puzzles. The distinguished lyricist and composer of the American stage Stephen Sondheim is also an ace puzzle constructor. Words and music go together like, well, like words in diagrams.

At some point, too, puzzle solvers realize they have style preferences. The *New York Times* crossword is the universal favorite. It is the standard by which all other American puzzles are measured. The main attraction is the crossword editor rather than any of the individual puzzle constructors who provide newspaper entertainment 365 days a year. Although a few hundred professional puzzle constructors contribute puzzles for publication, it is the editor who molds the outcome and leaves his or her mark on the clues.

Not only were my students at the New School eager to exchange ideas but they wanted to pose questions that had been bugging them for years. No matter where you fall on the spectrum of puzzles, you strive to move on to more advanced variations. For example, what is a *diagramless* puzzle? (It operates on clues alone.) How the heck do you solve a British crossword? (It requires an entirely different system of clues.) Our sessions were lively and full of opinions. Needless to say, puzzle solvers are a literate group, capable of finding how-to information on their own. But, with puzzles, it is helpful to have a demonstration.

Almost like traveling abroad, you encounter a different language in the puzzle world: Clues need to be translated into answers. Because of page-layout considerations, clues pack in lots of information in a minimum number of words. Like an urban home, the crossword stashes tons of stuff in a small space! For puzzle solvers and parents of teenagers, of which I happen to be both, posing one curt phrase to yield a one-word reply is second nature. If you can retain half of the few hundred four-letter combinations introduced in these pages, you will get along fine. For those who have a handle on this modern American dialect, this survey will be a reunion.

The benefits of puzzle solving have assumed new, amazing powers that are reminiscent of the fountain of youth. Yes, it is possible that a puzzle a day keeps the doctor away. The way I look at it, the activity is a mental workout that keeps your brain nimble in the way that push-ups keep your biceps firm. As the baby boomer generation reaches retirement age, anything that keeps their brains cooking is good news. I have even seen references in women's magazines that recommend puzzle solving as an appetite suppressant! The theory is that when absorbed with the clues, the puzzle solver is too busy to eat. Plus, puzzles keep your hands busy. So many good reasons to improve your puzzle-solving skills, even if only to add another string to your bow, as the British say to mean acquiring a new skill.

My Viennese-born father believed that the best way to learn a new language is to befriend a native speaker, which encourages chatting in your adopted tongue. Good advice—except in the case of Crosswordese because you won't use it to chat up anyone. As someone who has done serious time on both sides of the puzzle, I'm as close to a native speaker as you can get. Rather than focus on the big picture of puzzle solving, this book boils the game down to its smallest element. Like the Victorian drawing that contains two profiles—a young beauty or an old crone, depending on how your eye takes in the image—I draw your eye away from the long words for a closer look at my favorite four-letter words so you, too, can appreciate their true value. Along the way, I'll share some other insider insights gleaned from a life within the grid.

WHY FOUR-LETTER WORDS?
The Anatomy of a Crossword

*The attraction of solving a puzzle is the promise of
stumbling across a clue that will elicit a sudden laugh.*

NORMAN COUSINS, *SATURDAY REVIEW* EDITOR AND PUZZLE SOLVER

Rather than verbs, nouns, and their modifiers, communication inside crosswords requires **MEGA** (*puzzle clue:* "Large: pref.") doses of four-letter combinations. Without these little terms, the game could not exist. It is true that they were born outside the grid and originally functioned in the English vocabulary. The funny thing is that at this point they appear more often in crosswords than elsewhere. Absent from everyday chitchat, as a whole, they form a twenty-first-century dialect. Due to their symbiotic relationship with crosswords, puzzle constructors gang them together and refer to the lingo as *Crosswordese.* Although this term describes the three- to five-letter words that dominate the grid, the bulk of them consist of four letters. They are the bane of the puzzle constructor's profession because they are unoriginal and have turned into clichés. In fact, crossword editors try to limit their number per puzzle. To the puzzle solver, however, they are good news. They serve as stepping-stones into the grid and appear so frequently as to be labeled "repeaters" by people in the biz. Repeaters are the humdrum, predictable, bite-size fillers. In our times of radical change, there is some comfort in the way these old crossword puzzle friends greet us again and again.

When you look at the anatomy of what puzzle people refer to as a "conventional" or "daily" crossword, you see what a great fit four-letter words are in the white boxes. The crossword skeleton is a square grid of fifteen boxes across and down. Within the frame lie mainly white squares with a sprinkling of black ones, which vary in design from one crossword to another. To qualify as a professional puzzle, a crossword must fulfill half a dozen universal requirements:

- Every letter functions in two directions, Across and Down.

- Every answer is at least three letters long.

- The maximum number of words is seventy-eight.

- The maximum number of black boxes is thirty-eight.

- The pattern must be symmetrical (top mirrors bottom).

- The grid has an overall interlock so that no area is cut off.

In the jumbo Sunday crossword, the formula grows to accommodate a larger grid. Over the weekend, when puzzle solvers have more time to play, the puzzle typically swells to twenty-one boxes square. The bigger area accommodates 142 words and a maximum of seventy-four black squares. The absolute maximum size for a Sunday crossword is 23 × 23, which holds up to 170 words. Note that crossword grids always consist of an odd number of squares in order to accommodate the symmetrical pattern. The central line is unique, and the design above is mirrored below. Occasionally, editors allow clever exceptions to this pattern; but as a rule, puzzle solvers confront the standard formula.

The first order of business for a puzzle constructor is to choose a *theme* for the blank 15 × 15 diagram. Although it is not a requirement, the theme has evolved into the organizing principle of the game. This fancy word describes three long entries in a daily-size puzzle. These three answers are linked by a common idea that ties them together in a way that will help the puzzle solver guess the answers. Most often a theme appears in the Across (horizontal) boxes, ranging from twelve to fifteen letters per answer. Its purpose is to both tickle and challenge the puzzle solver. For example, a theme based on well-known comedy teams could include two fourteen-letter pairs such as **LAUREL AND HARDY** and **CHEECH AND CHONG** plus the fifteen-letter **THE THREE STOOGES** along the central horizontal. The average baby boomer recognizes the classic pair, Stan Laurel and Oliver Hardy; the slapstick Stooges, Moe, Larry, and Curly; as well as the pair of stars of the film *Up in Smoke* (1978). The answer words of these longer theme entries are all run-on in the grid, meaning there are no black squares between words. Placement is always symmetrical, with one answer in the center and the other two in parallel positions, most often four squares from the top and four from the bottom. Sometimes a daily crossword puzzle contains a theme of four answers. In this case, the answers are shorter at nine to eleven letters each. To accommodate four thematic answers, one pair may appear in parallel places Across and the other Down. In a Sunday puzzle, a theme may include six to eight related answers. As a rule, themed answers appear Across more often than Down.

The next step for the puzzle constructor is to insert the theme letters into their assigned boxes from left to right. In the sample case, the comedy teams take up forty-three squares. One black box introduces a fourteen-letter entry, while the other ends with one. Now the balance of the boxes remains to be filled with random words. That is the biggest part of the puzzle constructor's job because all the letters belong to words that read in two directions. Technically, these words represent the "fill," which is truth in labeling. Although the theme is the fun and chuckle-worthy part of puzzle solving, the fill dominates the diagram. It consists of the words that go into the rest of the blanks.

No matter how a puzzle constructor tries to keep them to a minimum, so-called repeaters hold up the puzzle corners. Like back-up singers, they make the star look good. With the three theme entries spanning Across, the puzzle creator carves up the grid. Across the top line, a standard crossword features three columns Across with black squares between. The pattern is often a pair of four-letter words and one of five letters, in any sequence. The same pattern is mirrored at the bottom of the diagram. Typically, these are groups of four-letter words in both sections interlocking with other four-letter words. On closer scrutiny, it is a gold mine of repeaters.

Automatically, the seasoned solver gravitates to repeater clues to gain entry into the grid. It's not too strenuous to match standard clues to their answers as with **ABBA** for *puzzle clue:* "Swedish rock group," the one and only in puzzledom; **BETA** as in *puzzle clue:* "Phi — Kappa"; and **FALA** for *puzzle clue:* "FDR's pet," his beloved Scottish terrier. One common characteristic of these three particular repeaters is their final **A**. All of these are comfortable either Across or Down. Their letters lend themselves to crisscrossing with other short words, so that they dovetail seamlessly.

Secondary clues for these repeaters include *puzzle clue:* "Statesman Eban" of Israel (**ABBA**) and *puzzle clue:* "Word with blocker" (**BETA**). Puzzle constructors have no choice for FDR's best friend. By changing his dog's name from Big Boy to **FALA** (short for Murray the Outlaw of Falahill), President Roosevelt guaranteed that crosswords would make his terrier immortal alongside the other perennial puzzle pup from the 1930s detective comedy, uniquely named **ASTA**, *puzzle clue:* "'The Thin Man' pet."

Depending on their position in the grid, repeaters favor different letter combinations. Across the upper left you are more likely to see repeaters that feature two or even three consonants, and **E** will be the least popular vowel. This is due to the nature of English spelling. Typical top-row crossword entries include **TARA** (*puzzle clue:* "Scarlett's home" from *Gone with the Wind*), **NAPA** (*puzzle clue:* "Sonoma County neighbor"), and **ALAN** (*puzzle clue:* "Actor Alda"). Across the bottom of the grid, repeaters are heavier on **D**, **E**, **R**, and **S**. These are the letters that dominate the end of words. Here you bump into

DELE (*puzzle clue:* "Remove from a text") and **SERE** (*puzzle clue:* "Like the Sahara") or its homonym **SEER** (*puzzle clue:* "Clairvoyant"). What repeaters have no use for are the letters **F, J, K, Q, V, W,** and **Z**. Not that they will disappear from the game, but they are the exception. Because these letters are more difficult to interlock, they don't belong in the roster of common four-letter words.

▪ ▪▪ ▪

As with any language, the language of crosswords requires a certain amount of rote memorization. Take the morbid-looking *puzzle clue:* "Dies —," for example. On first glance, this looks to be an English phrase. *Dies* plus four letters? Sounds so James Bond, but resist that impulse. Bad news is banished from crosswords because the game is intended to divert and entertain. You will not see a crossword about ailments. In light of this, pronounce **DIES** in two syllables as *dee-ess*. With experience, the scholar of Crosswordese shifts to Latin. Yes, think Gregorian chant or "Dies **IRAE**" (Day of Wrath), the hymn that plays a major role in the Roman Catholic Church. Describing the day of reckoning or judgment, many scholars consider it to be the best example of Medieval Latin poetry. It inspired Mozart, Verdi, and Berlioz to compose their requiems and continues to make appearances in modern plays and even pop music. The poem begins: "*Dies irae, dies illa.*" But never mind, all you need to know is the second word: **IRAE**. Do solvers care about how pleased puzzle constructors are that the genitive case in Latin puts **A** before **E**?

Scribbling four-letter repeaters into the grid without much brain strain is the reward for years of puzzle practice. Expert puzzle solvers anticipate them, seek them out, secretly welcome them when they intersect with a tricky answer, and know they make unraveling the theme entries easier. They mutter other four-letter words when they can't match a clue to the repeater. The key to success is the ability to identify a repeater in order to confidently write in the pristine white boxes. Scan the clues for other repeaters and pretty soon you have completed a nice chunk.

Beginner puzzle solvers tend to approach crosswords as a team sport, asking anyone within earshot for help—as in, "What is the first name of author Silverstein?" Fans of his picture book *The Giving Tree* instantly reply, "**SHEL**" (short for *Shelby*). The nickname registers in the memory bank as the only Shel in the puzzle universe (or perhaps outside). Once you read the book, the tale of the relationship between a tree and a boy, you will never forget how hard it is to read out loud to the end without getting choked up. The work languished in manuscript for four years until editor Ursula Nordstrom took the plunge and published it in 1964, sad ending in tact. Nordstrom authored one of my childhood favorites: *The Secret Language*, about two girls with their own private dialect, budding puzzle solvers.

Depending on who edits the *New York Times* crossword, the lexicon of repeaters shifts. Repeaters go in and out of fashion. Once upon a time, solvers encountered the opaque *puzzle clue:* "Hebrew month" with predictable frequency. What's worse, there are two four-letter Hebrew months! Outside of subscribers to the *Jerusalem Times*, can the average solver distinguish **ADAR** from **ELUL**? Each lasts twenty-nine days, alternating with months of thirty days, and derives from the Babylonian. Not that it matters, provided you remember the pair of four-letter candidates that answer the *puzzle clue:* "Hebrew month." A good speller will bet on **ADAR** for the way its letters dovetail with interlocking words. As *Wheel of Fortune* viewers note, **E** may be top in popularity, but Vanna turns over **A**, **D**, and **R** way more often than **L** and **U**.

■ ■ ■

When learning any language, you need to exercise your limited vocabulary to retain proper usage. To find repeaters, eyeball the Across and Down list for the key clue categories outlined here. As a solver, I follow this particular sequence for best results, and it works well while you're getting your bearings in the crossword. There's time to ramp up the challenge later in life. Get out your pen and see if you can solve for the telltale dashes of what I'll call the missing links in the first list of clues. If your strong suit is dictionary definitions or proper names, the second or third list of repeaters is for you. The trickiest group is the foreign words; unless you have them memorized, save these for last.

Missing Links: Easy to Identify by the Giveaway Dash

Puzzle clue: "Jai —" for **ALAI**, the sport popular in Florida

Puzzle clue: "'—, poor Yorick'" for **ALAS**, from Shakespeare

Puzzle clue: "'— Lang Syne'" for **AULD**, from the New Year's Eve anthem

Puzzle clue: "— vera" for **ALOE**, the healing plant

Puzzle clue: "Phi — Kappa" for **BETA**, the fraternity

Puzzle clue: "Or —!" for **ELSE**, the threatening ultimatum

Puzzle clue: "Pro —" for **RATA**, the stockholder's term

Puzzle clue: "— Hashanah" for **ROSH**, the Jewish holiday

Puzzle clue: "— of the D'Urbervilles" for **TESS**, the Thomas Hardy heroine

Puzzle clue: "— Bator," for **ULAN**, the Asian country

Dictionary Definitions: Straight from *Webster's*, Rarely Heard in Polite (or Any) Company

Puzzle clue: "To shelter, nautically" for **ALEE**, the sailor's term

Puzzle clue: "Seed cover" for **ARIL**, the farmer's term

Puzzle clue: "Dueling sword" for **EPEE**, the modern pentathlete's term

Puzzle clue: "Anglo-Saxon slave" for **ESNE**, the laborer

Puzzle clue: "Decorative case" for **ETUI**, the seamstress's term

Puzzle clue: "Brain passage" for **ITER**, the neurosurgeon's term

Puzzle clue: "Kind of tide" for **NEAP**, the astronomer's term

Puzzle clue: "Hawaiian goose" for **NENE**, the bird

Puzzle clue: "Curved molding" for **OGEE**, the architect's term

Puzzle clue: "Ankle bones" for **TALI**, the anatomical term

Proper Names: People You Meet Mainly Through Crosswords

Puzzle clue: "Architect Saarinen" for **EERO**, the Finn

Puzzle clue: "Director Kazan" for **ELIA**, who directed *East of Eden*

Puzzle clue: "Author Wiesel" for **ELIE**, the Nobel Prize winner

Puzzle clue: "Witty Bombeck" for **ERMA**, the humorist

Puzzle clue: "Morales of *NYPD Blue*" for **ESAI**, the actor

Puzzle clue: "Composer Stravinsky" for **IGOR**, who wrote *The Firebird*

Puzzle clue: "Tennis player Nastase" for **ILIE**, the Romanian ace

Puzzle clue: "Architect van der Rohe" for Ludwig **MIES**, the German-born American

Puzzle clue: "Patron saint of Norway" for **OLAV**, the Viking king

Puzzle clue: "Mrs. Chaplin" for **OONA**, who married Charlie

Puzzle clue: "Author Silverstein" for **SHEL**, who wrote *The Giving Tree*

Foreign Words: A Cross Section from Many Lands

Puzzle clue: "Asian governess" for **AMAH**, from Chinese

Puzzle clue: "Latin 101 verb" for **AMAT**, from Latin

Puzzle clue: "Part of A.D." for **ANNO**, from Latin

Puzzle clue: "Hombre's home" for **CASA**, from Spanish

Puzzle clue: "Hamburger's home" for **HAUS**, from German

Puzzle clue: "Dies —" for **IRAE**, from Latin

Puzzle clue: "Film category" for **NOIR**, from French

Puzzle clue: "Hindu princess" for **RANI**, from India

Puzzle clue: "Drink with sushi" for **SAKE**, from Japan

Puzzle clue: "French thinker?" for **TETE**, from French

For our purposes we can dispense with the two remaining types of crossword clues—namely wordplay and themes. Traditionally, these glamorous categories eclipse repeaters with their intrinsic flair, but no longer. **LITE** (*puzzle clue:* "Low-cal") words are about to step into the limelight.

2

Decoding Clues:
How to Solve for Four-Letter Words

When my mind is on the puzzle, I can't worry about what
Congress is going to do with the new tax bill.

LOUIS RUKEYSER, *WALL STREET WEEK* HOST AND PUZZLE SOLVER

If you are really going to feel comfortable using Crosswordese,
you need a little background about how the code works. Just
like a studio apartment in midtown Manhattan, this little
space holds a lot of stuff. But you have to know where to look.
You know the layout: A 15 × 15 square plan with five-sixths
consisting of white squares. No trespassing into the one-sixth
(or fewer) black squares, much like those no-go closet zones
that most of us never get around to sorting. About thirty-
eight numbered boldface clues in each direction, Across and
Down, of which one-quarter or more may be four-letter words.

A good many of these words begin with vowels and alternate vowel-consonant-vowel-consonant.

By dint of space issues, clues are short. Paper costs are forever going up and newspapers would rather sell ads than chop down more trees to make more room for the crossword. Even if that were not the case, puzzle people would communicate economically because we are environmentally aware, right? In truth, each word functions in multiple ways. As a result, a one-word clue is not unusual. For example, *puzzle clue:* "Lure" (**BAIT**). In a G-rated atmosphere, resist the sexy connotation of lure as a verb and opt for its definition as a noun. Think fishing. You might cast in a *puzzle clue:* "Streamlet" (**RILL**). Another to-the-point example is *puzzle clue:* "Copycat," which yields the age-old repeater **APER**. In Crosswordese, **APE** is a verb rather than a noun, so "Copy" or "Imitate" is the clue that elicits **APE**. If you go ape, you follow the leader in this game.

Stay on the lookout for double entendres. If you see what appears as a straightforward one-word puzzle clue like "Carol" with a four-letter answer, resist the impulse to connect the name with a celebrity such as songwriter King (given name Carole with an **E**). Because the clue begins with an upper-case letter, the assumption is that the word is part of a name. Move away from pop culture and look at the word with a lower-case **C**, as in Christmas carol, or the four-letter word **NOEL**.

A **SNAP** (*puzzle clue:* "Cinch") once you know how to decipher properly. Also beware its verb form, when **SNAP** answers to a puzzle clue like "Go postal."

■ □ ■

Like French with its double negatives or Japanese with its verb at the end of the sentence, you have to know how to scan Crosswordese. Use the following shortcuts to decipher four basic types of repeaters and give yourself the upper hand on clue structure. The system follows a logical pattern—once you understand a few key indicators.

Abbreviations

What's the story with abbreviations? For the most part, you find the puzzle clue tagged with a colon and the obvious four letters with capital **A**, "Abbr." For example, *puzzle clue:* "Wall Street institution: Abbr." emerges as the acronym **NYSE** (New York Stock Exchange). Clear-cut puzzle clues like "Pilot's concerns: Abbr." result in the useful **ALTS** (the plural abbreviation for *altitudes*). A plural clue yields a plural answer. **ALT** in the singular is linked with *puzzle clue:* "Supermodel Carol," ranked in the top ten of famous cover girls. Don't dust off another high-rise repeater removed by one consonant, **ALPS**, the most popular of which is *puzzle clue:* "— Blanc" (**MONT**). Sometimes the mountain appears with a French twist as

ALPE. Alternatively, Mont Blanc is the brand name for a top-of-the-line fountain pen, prized possession of ink solvers everywhere. But I digress.

Nowadays, the tag is just as often omitted, and the abbreviation is implied through the clue structure. A missing colon should not throw you: The tip-off is an abbreviation within the clue, which signals that the answer is an abbreviation. In this scenario **NYSE** matches *puzzle clue:* "Wall Street inst." (the last four letters are short for *institution*). **SASE** (self-addressed stamped envelope) answers to "Ms. enclosure," in which the "Ms." is short for the word *manuscript* rather than the American honorific for a woman. *Puzzle clue:* "US WWII ally" comes up **USSR**. The Soviet Union is gone but not forgotten, thanks to the useful consonants **SSR**, which march on in crosswords. Continuing with the theme of World War II, there is the repeater **DDAY** for *puzzle clue:* "WWII turning point." What other repeater begins with double **D** and ends in **Y**? Its unique spelling ensures its long life as a four-letter word.

Institutions produce massive numbers of four-letter terms. Start with coursework, *puzzle clue:* "MBA subject," which could be **ECON** (economics). Or, less often, **TRIG** (trigonometry). *Puzzle clue:* "Univ. course" favors **ECOL** (ecology). "Med school subject" is predictably **ANAT** (anatomy). What else do MDs need to know besides anatomy? Possibly **BIOL** (biology). Schools like **UCLA** (*puzzle clue:* "Campus NW of LA") make good fodder. The government is also repeater rich: "B-52 org." for **USAF** (United States Air Force) and "Letters before prime" (**USDA**) make for useful combinations. **OSHA** (*puzzle clue:* "Dept of Labor division" or "Fed. watchdog"), short for the Occupational Safety and Health Administration, probably leads the pack.

Once you work out the way abbreviations generate abbreviations, the time comes to check for code terms that convey this concept. Key phrases include *in short, for short, briefly,* and *informally,* all telegraphing the notion that the answer will be curtailed. For the same answers listed above you may see *puzzle clues:* "Department of Labor division, in short," "B-52 organization, briefly," and "Intern's course, for short," for **OSHA**, **USAF**, and **ANAT**, respectively. It's the constructor's way of keeping your interest while feeding you the same old repeaters.

Disguising abbreviations this way is adopted from the British crossword code. Every single clue in the British puzzle is a form of riddle that adheres to a shorthand system, so don't feel sorry for yourself. It is symptomatic of the circuitous way the British communicate, unlike the straight-talking American—isn't that so; cheerio, old chap; and **TATA**?

Word Parts

Due to the limited pool of acceptable four-letter words available to puzzle constructors, repeaters feed on prefixes and suffixes. As with abbreviations, when constructors are benevolent, the clue comes tagged and wrapped in a bow, as with *puzzle clue:* "Prefix with gram" (**TELE**). Or the clue may appear in dictionary form as "Distant: prefix." Same goes for **ALTI**, which might be *puzzle clue:* "Prefix with meter" or "High: prefix." Thanks to strides in electronics, **TELE** has a new definition as "HDTV component." If you keep up-to-date with your flat-screen high-definition TV, you will have the answer.

Two prefixes with history in crosswords are at opposite ends of the spectrum: **ENDO** (*puzzle clue:* "Prefix with skeleton") and **ECTO** (*puzzle clue:* "Prefix with morph"). One means "inner," the other means "outer." It doesn't matter if you keep them straight provided that you match them with the correct clue. Some prefixes have become stand-alone words. The word **MAXI** is currently defined by *puzzle clue:* "Big, in adspeak," whereas **MINI** and **MIDI** can answer "Skirt style." Style includes technology: For the freshest clue for **MINI**, try *puzzle clue:* "Certain iPod."

Borrowing again from the British clue shorthand, the current American clue reference to a prefix includes the key words *start* and *opener*, whereas *ending* signals a suffix. Following this logic, **AERO** answers *puzzle clue:* "Space opener"; **MEGA** *puzzle clue:* "The start of something big"; and **STER** *puzzle clue:* "Trick ending." Cute!

The Internet is producing new repeater candidates, such as *puzzle clue:* "Web address lead-in" (**HTTP**, for hypertext transfer protocol) and "Web programmer's medium" (**HTML**, for hypertext markup language), completely new consonant combinations. The jury is still out on whether these unexpected strings of consonants lend themselves to the lexicon of repeaters or whether website designers will come up with better vowel-rich acronyms.

Two Words

Short phrases feed the lexicon of four-letter words. They run together in the grid, so in the early days constructors tagged them. One example is *puzzle clue:* "Sale sign: two wds." for **ASIS**, the retailer's warning that a discounted item has a fatal flaw like a dress with a broken zipper. Current constructors drop the tag, putting the **ONUS** (*puzzle clue:* "Responsibility") on the solver. So you find the answer to *puzzle clues:* "Massive amount" is **ATON** and "Each" is the slangy term **APOP**. Some phrases offer two possible responses, as in *puzzle clue:* "Regarding," which is either **ASTO** or **INRE**.

For umpteen years Sammy Davis Jr. received valuable free publicity with the title of his autobiography, "Yes, —" (**ICAN**). Sammy trumped the song line, "Anything you can do, — do better." I never read his book, but I will never forget the title. Now the entry also answers to *puzzle clue:* "Volunteer's phrase."

The other **I** repeater with amazing staying power is the answer to *puzzle clue:* "Understanding phrase" or "Gotcha!" (**ISEE**).

Colloquialisms fall into the missing-link category. As missing links, two words offer easy entree into the grid. Sayings that you know as well as you know your own name fall into this category. George Washington's fateful admission "I cannot tell —" (**ALIE**). The hot retort "Thanks —!" (**ALOT**). The axiom "— first you don't succeed" (**IFAT**). And one place you don't want to be with crosswords, *puzzle clue:* "Stuck in —" (**ARUT**).

Fill in the blank for "Me, myself —," and you get **ANDI**. In olden days, this phrase was clued by the 1945 bestseller by Betty MacDonald, *The Egg and I,* about a city girl who marries a chicken farmer out in the boondocks of Washington State. The film inspired the spin-off of the classic Ma and Pa Kettle series. Then there is the classic call to Mother in *puzzle clue:* "Look —!" (**ATME**). Or the big spender's remark, *puzzle clue:* "It's —" (**ONME**). Not to mention that remark before an explosion, "You're getting —!" (**TOME**). Or self-pity, *puzzle clue:* "Words of woe" (**AHME**). Then there is the Beatles hit of 1964, "Love —" (**MEDO**). Yes, it always comes back to **ME**.

Question Marks

Grammar has no place in the world of four-letter words. But questions in clues do. When you see a question mark, prepare yourself for a clever turn of phrase that is dressing up an otherwise stale repeater. In code, a question mark means the answer is not what you expect. For *puzzle clue:* "Major finale?" interpret the word *finale* as a synonym for *ender*, the code for a suffix, as in the repeater **ETTE**.

Once again, the British sense of humor influences the clue structure for these posers. You have to suspend judgment rather than read the question literally. "Way off base?" is a tongue-in-cheek puzzle clue for **AWOL**. *Off base* is not meant in the colloquial sense but is a literal reference. Without the question mark, you would be dealing with the words *off base* in the sense of wrong or off the mark. The four-letter term that is short for "absent without leave" describes a way of getting off the base. The answer to *puzzle clue:* "Soft rock?" is **LAVA**, the material used for pumice stones and not **LITE** music as aired on the AM radio.

When you get the hang of how to read the question and interpret its elements, you will gain a sense of accomplishment when that light bulb goes off in your head.

▬ ▬ ▬

Jim Fixx, a world-famous athlete and author of the bestselling *Complete Book of Running* (1977), is considered the leader of the fitness movement that swept the United States in the last half of the twentieth century. His fifteen-mile-a-day run was widely documented, but his research in mental gymnastics is less well known. Always fascinated by the extent of human endurance, he was an expert in logic puzzles. Years before he promoted running, Fixx compiled a series of books called *Games for the Super-Intelligent* and a children's version called *Solve It!* As he told me in a discussion about puzzles, the idea struck him after he researched an article on the so-called genius club called Mensa. Two British barristers established the society shortly after World War II. They named it Mensa, Latin for "table," because their intention was to begin a round-table for sociable folks with above-average intelligence who were seeking like-minded company. To join Mensa, prospective members take an IQ test; those who score in the top 2 percentile are accepted.

Mensa did not cross the Atlantic until 1961. Although men joined up (among them Fixx himself), they were outnumbered by American women, who leapt at the opportunity for mental stimulation in those days before women's liberation, according to Fixx. He found one common thread among Mensa members: a serious attraction to puzzles. There was a huge appetite for logic questions with tricky replies, much like British crossword clues. Brain teasers may seem frivolous, but this puzzle expert saw the serious underside: At the end of our interview for the *New York Herald Tribune Crosswords*, he told me, "Working out the answer is an oblique lesson in how to solve real-life problems."

Fixx's theory was that word games allow the mind to do its best work. He surmised that the brain needs time to marinate ideas. He told me that the mind does not work in a linear way, "which is why business meetings are such a bore. Solutions come from different directions, which are the reasons why getting out on the track or working a puzzle gives the mind the freedom to be creative."

3

The First Lady of Four-Letter Words:
Margaret Farrar née Petherbridge

Do puzzles.

JACQUES LACAN, FATHER OF FRENCH PSYCHOLOGY AND PUZZLE SOLVER

With a crossword in every newspaper nowadays, it's hard to believe that during World War I only New Yorkers had access to the puzzle. A transplanted Liverpudlian by the name of Arthur Wynne had devised a one-off for the Fun section of the *New York World* as a Christmas treat in 1913. When Wynne's readers demanded an encore, he complied every Sunday. Readers sent in their work, which set the precedent for the current system of freelance submissions polished by an in-house editor. For ten years Wynne limped along, patching together a "cross word," growing more frustrated with the production nightmare of missing clues and mismatched numbers that plagued the crossword in its early days.

Because the crossword is stitched together with many little boxes, it was not unusual for clue numbers to fall off the page or get pasted into the wrong box. In the typesetting process, sometimes clues were left out altogether. Crosswords have so many moving parts that it's understandable how mistakes could appear in the pre-computer process of newspaper production. At issue was the lack of quality assurance and review for the crossword puzzle before it went to press. With great relief, the newspaperman handed over the chaotic department to his energetic assistant, Margaret. His stepdaughter's roommate at Smith College, Margaret Petherbridge arrived after walking out on a banking job that did not draw on her considerable talents. The last straw at the bank was a request to file "Coty Frères" under **F** for *Frères*, which means "brothers" in French, rather than **C** for the surname *Coty*. She was just the sort of stickler that the *World* needed to look after its unkempt crossword puzzle.

Little did Wynne anticipate how delegating this responsibility would result in crossword fever, giving newspapers around the world a selling point that would become a permanent feature as readers discovered a new reason to buy the paper.

By the time I had the pleasure of meeting Petherbridge in 1979, she had become Mrs. Farrar, the puzzle powerhouse whose scientific attention to the crossword ended up creating a multimillion-dollar category for the publishing industry in the 1920s. By 1930, she had moved from the *New York World* to set up, produce, and supervise the crossword division of Simon & Schuster. In 1942, she introduced the crossword puzzle to the *New York Times*, and upon leaving that post in 1969, she started a syndicated crossword puzzle for the *Los Angeles Times.* Keeping puzzle solvers amused was her nonstop occupation.

My entree to her was a complaint addressed to Eugene Sheffer, care of King Features, for which she had been sent a carbon copy ("cc") at the *Los Angeles Times.* (Those good old days of carbon copies, the black sheets inserted behind the original, which left black smudges all over your fingers.) An irate solver in Denver had taken fifteen years off from the sport and, like Rip van Winkle, woke up to a changed world. "Your puzzles are destroying the educational premise of the crossword puzzle," harrumphed this critic. She was harking to the days when Latin was the lingua franca of crossword puzzles, and **ERGO** she fully expected to see Caesar's legacy. She required more of **AMAT** (*puzzle clue:* "Amo, amas, —"; I love, you love, he loves) and **VIDI** (*puzzle clue:* "Veni, —, vici" or "I came, I saw, I conquered," as Caesar remarked after the Battle of Zela in 47 BCE). Instead, she encountered such transgressions as four-letter word **EDEN** defined as " 'I Dream of Jeannie' star Barbara." On the heels of this complaint, a typewritten note on graph paper arrived on my desk from Farrar herself. "This is a diatribe about the current state of affairs. It could spark a very lively discussion. Do give me a ring some evening."

At issue was whether slang and pop culture have a place in crosswords. They entered the roster of four-letter words surreptitiously and are now full-fledged members. The question of crosswords as a learning tool or a general knowledge game is an ongoing debate, with each camp standing firm, although the latter has gained the upper hand. Will Shortz, leader of the 1980s faction then known as the "New Wave," is full steam ahead on incorporating colloquialisms, brand names, and all things current into the grid. Four-letter words that appear in the pages of the *Times* are welcome in today's crossword. This philosophy is counter to that of his predecessor, Eugene T. Maleska, the educator and third crossword editor at the *New York Times*, who considered the crossword as a mini classroom and shunned contemporary terms.

How far puzzles have come since that fateful day in 1923 when Wynne relinquished the drawer full of grids and puzzles to young Petherbridge! Sheffer urged me to follow up with the

"Grande Dame" of crosswords, as he called the editor to whom he made his first puzzle sale in 1920. A telephone call turned into an invitation for tea at her Upper East Side apartment. Every horizontal space was covered by piles of books, fireplace included. She led me to a clear space, explaining that with so many puzzles to test solve, she had no time for anything else.

The dynamic editor, who in 1923 personally assumed the duty of quality assurance for the *New York World* crossword puzzle, had devised the concept of test-solving puzzle contributions. Consistently, over half a century, she proofread the crosswords in her care before they went to print. This was a complete turnaround from her cynical first days on staff, when she scoffed at letters about errors in the weekly crossword. Who besides a crank, she thought, could take the time to write about a silly game? Keeping errors out of crosswords is a task of Sisyphean proportion, and solvers are a demanding lot when their favorite pastime is concerned, as those in the field well know.

One high-profile solver to give Farrar a hard time about typos was the widely read newspaperman Franklin P. Adams, aka "FPA," who produced a regular column called "The Conning Tower." (The term refers to a platform on a battleship that allows the officer to survey the vessel and direct the helmsman.) When his office moved next door to hers, FPA subjected the puzzle editor to relentless teasing. The way she recalled it, he formed the irritating habit of stalking in every Monday morning at about 11 to point out in sarcastic tones just what was wrong with the crossword from the day before. Dreading another such drubbing, she finally picked up her pencil to solve a copy of the upcoming puzzle. As she became frustrated by missing numbers and omitted clues, the penny dropped.

At that very minute, she vowed on her *Webster's* to uphold the quality of the crossword, she later recalled. From that date onward she checked the proof of the Fun section's puzzle before it was published. If she saw numbers in wrong boxes or found that clues were missing, she corrected them on the proof and marched the emended puzzle over to the copy desk. She made certain that the corrections were made before the crossword saw the light of day. FPA was not the only puzzle solver to appreciate her hard work: Within a matter of months, she turned a typesetter's nightmare into an international craze.

■ ■ ■ ■

Having tamed the wild crossword, Farrar (then Petherbridge) received an intriguing request from two new graduates of Columbia University School of Journalism. (At this point in the tale of crosswords, puzzle-minded readers may have noted the starring role that Columbia University has played in its development. The other key player in crossword-puzzle evolution is the state of Indiana, having produced both Wills: Weng and Shortz, second and fourth crossword editors at the *New York Times*.) The pair of Columbians, a Mr. Simon and a Mr. Schuster, were thinking about issuing a compilation of crosswords. The brainstorm struck when, according to the apocryphal publishing tale, an aunt of one of the young men told him about the futile search for such a book at Christmas. When she came up empty-handed, she appealed for his help. She thought it would make the ideal gift for her daughter.

To meet a pressing deadline, the enterprising Farrar recruited two colorfully named colleagues: Prosper "Pros" Buranelli, a feature writer, and F. Gregory "Gregorian" Hartswick, the cryptogram editor at the *World*. (Cryptograms are sentences written in a scrambled alphabet code so that each letter represents another one.) Each editor received an advance of $25, a fair amount for that era. When asked if he would provide an introduction, Farrar's in-house critic, FPA, declined. He then spent many days in the doorway of her office, trying to talk her out of the project. No one anticipated how this slim $1.35 volume, including Venus pencil, would become the best seller that launched the giant publishing house of Simon & Schuster. With the virtual overnight success of *The Cross Word Puzzle Book*, Farrar set to work on the series that established her as a household name.

In that first year, Simon & Schuster kept the presses running with three volumes of crosswords flying off the shelves at the rate of hundreds of thousands. At the holidays, the books topped most shopping lists: a record 150,000 copies sold on a single shopping day in December 1924. As the story ends, Aunt Wixie, the relative who had sparked the project, received her copy hot off the presses for her puzzle-loving daughter. Farrar had her doubts about Wixie's role in the process, but there was no doubt about her own role in the future development of the craze.

An industry was born, and the Simon & Schuster puzzle series continues unbroken.

◼ ◼ ◼

As the creator and popularizer of the modern crossword puzzle, literally the brain that devised the rules, Farrar was circumspect about the complainer from Denver seeking educational words in her puzzle solving. "Crosswords are intended to be good fun," remained her mantra. Fun does not preclude learning or the use of references. However, it can be compromised by predictability. The well of four-letter words drains quickly. Puzzle constructors curse repeaters, because they compromise originality. No matter how often the puzzle editor plucks them out, they grow back because their letters interlock so neatly with the longer intersecting entries.

English spelling favors certain letter combinations, which is where the frustration lies.

That's why Farrar welcomed the expansion of essential Crosswordese. After decades of test solving, she understood firsthand how repetitious the process was. She craved more than a diet of **ERNE** (*puzzle clue:* "Coastal flier") and **ABED** (*puzzle clue:* "Retired"). Her stable of puzzle constructors came to the rescue. Farrar credited Maleska (third editor of the *Times* crossword) with introducing the concept of run-on four-letter phrases into the grid. Puzzle solvers are now unfazed to encounter the odd looking **ASIS** in answer to *puzzle clue:* "Words on a sales tag."

Slang was the next frontier to enrich the puzzle vocabulary. *Puzzle clue:* "Beat it!" commonly appears for either **SCAT** or **SHOO**. Crosswordese has come to include words that even take experienced solvers by surprise. By 2007, pop culture had changed so drastically from the prior century that puzzle clues with movie references such as "Subject of 'The Last King of Scotland'" and "Extra in 'The Producers'" yield two formerly banished four-letter words in the grid—namely **AMIN** and **NAZI**. Not that either one qualifies for standard Crosswordese, but they illustrate how far the puzzle constructor reaches to engage the solving audience.

The goal of the crossword editor, as outlined by Farrar,

is to provide a pastime from which a solver emerges feeling refreshed and accomplished. *Good Housekeeping* ran a feature on the woman it dubbed "the Queen of Crosswords" soon after she launched the *Times* crossword over sixty years ago. A typical workday in the life of Margaret Farrar was described as beginning at 10 p.m., when her brood of three was **ABED**. The hush of predawn New York City set the tone Farrar needed for concentration. Traveling to the *New York Times* office from the Upper East Side by bus in the afternoons, fellow passengers came to recognize her by the omnipresent puzzle proofs on her lap. She welcomed their input, and puzzle solvers applauded her for turning crosswords into entertainment rather than a measure of their spelling skills. As for herself, she modestly observed, the reward had been a ragbag vocabulary. Call it ragbag or reward, it is the knowledge that the puzzle solver needs in order to ace the crossword.

EGAD! In 1969, Farrar was forced to step down from her command post at the *New York Times* crossword. Human resources discovered that she had passed the mandatory retirement age of seventy by two years. Young Margaret Petherbridge of the *New York World* during the Roaring Twenties had become Mrs. Farrar by the 1960s, establishing the *Times* puzzle as the standard against which all American acrossionados are and shall forever be measured. Pressed for a replacement, human resources cast about for an in-house candidate.

Only one man on the premises of the *Times* had exhibited an aptitude for four-letter words of the crossword variety, and he was head of the metro desk. As the sole employee with experience in puzzles, Will Weng gamely (no better adverb) accepted the post of second crossword editor at the *New York Times*.

4

FOUR-LETTER WORDS IN THE *NEW YORK TIMES*:
All the Puzzles That Are Printed to Fit

When I was hired at the *New York Times*, I would measure my
mental alertness by picking up a ballpoint with one hand
and a lit cigarette in the other. If I could finish both at the
same time, I knew I was on the ball. After I quit smoking, it
became harder to measure my mental powers.

RUSSELL BAKER, PULITZER PRIZE–WINNING AUTHOR AND PUZZLE SOLVER

Getting a job at the *New York Times* turned Russell Baker into
an acrossionado. The way he recounted the sequence of events
to me during our chat about puzzle solving, he just couldn't
leave the space empty on the page. He started with the conventional crossword and went on to the hard stuff, the crossword variations at the bottom of the Sunday *Times* magazine
puzzle page. Ink is his solving medium of choice. When he

makes the occasional mistake, he scribbles over the wrong letter, which makes for a "colorful" page. His excuse for spending so much time with puzzles is that they turn the brain on. For someone whose business is words, that's a good thing.

When solvers ask about "the puzzle," as in "Did you do the puzzle today?" it is understood that the question refers to the one in the *Times*. Most often the question comes up on a Sunday. On the traditional day of rest, the puzzle takes up half a page in the back of the *New York Times Magazine* and requires a significant time commitment. Even the most speedy puzzle solver needs thirty minutes to be able to read clues, interpret them, and fill in the answers. Although the everyday crossword measures fifteen squares Across and Down, on Sunday it supersizes to twenty-one squares or, tops, twenty-three squares. Other brands simply do not warrant discussion because no other single puzzle is attacked by millions of people, predictably on the same day within hours of each other, and provokes or inspires so much commentary.

Fellow *Times* solvers instantly fathom the reason for the question, be it a clever theme that stumped them (albeit briefly) or a surprise message in the grid. Instead of spelling out card suits, for example, perhaps the constructor inserted a "rebus," or picture icon for clubs, hearts, spades, or diamonds in one answer box. When you're a **TYRO** (*puzzle clues:* "Beginner," "Newbie," and "Recruit, to Caesar"), you develop your basic skills by working any puzzle in the hundreds of puzzle magazines on the newsstand. At no extra cost, you can practice on the puzzle page of a local newspaper. But once you have earned your stripes, you tackle the *New York Times*. Even when you're traveling abroad you can get your daily dose of the *Times* crossword from the *International Herald Tribune*, a wholly owned subsidiary. Puzzles can now be accessed and printed out from websites in our computerized world. But how can you compare the clinical pressing of a button for a printout to the thrill of newsprint-covered fingers as you flip through the pages, past advertisements for holiday sales to the familiar black-and-white grid?

Thousands of newspapers get their crossword supply from syndicates like King Features, which was founded by William Randolph Hearst in 1915. That is where I started out as assistant to Eugene Sheffer thirty years ago. Nothing wrong with that puzzle! While it satisfies the puzzle appetite, the *Times* crossword contingent pledges allegiance to the editor. As a clue stylist, the editor's personality is the clincher for the committed puzzle solver. Even though the material is submitted by freelance puzzle constructors, by imbuing the clues with that *Times* flavor, and in the process rewriting at least half of them, the crossword editor engages in a dialogue with the solving audience. It is that extra dimension that turns a casual interest into a daily habit. Editor Margaret Farrar set the tone when she introduced the crossword feature in the *New York Times* in 1942, and her three successors have continued the tradition.

Seasoned solvers are well aware that the *New York Times* calibrates its crossword so that it escalates in challenge from Monday onward. Starting the workweek presents enough of a hurdle without a kick in the teeth from the puzzle, which is why Monday's is gentlest. Chances are you will find more Crosswordese in the puzzle earlier in the week, which offers a good opportunity to practice your four-letter-word vocabulary. At the end of the week, you are pressed to flex your mental muscle. Seasoned puzzle solvers, with their fluency in the lingo, save their ink for Wednesday or, for the more flamboyant, Thursday.

▄ ▄ ▄

When did the *New York Times* consider crosswords fit to print? Not until publisher Arthur Hays Sulzberger developed a taste for solving. Hard to believe that a pastime that seems to have been around for **EONS** (*puzzle clue:* "Long time") did not appear on the scene until **FDR** (*puzzle clue:* "Monogram before HST") was in the White House. The year was 1941 when Sulzberger came to the conclusion that he would no longer rely on the then-rival *Herald Tribune* for its puzzle. The first step was a telephone call to the First Lady of Crosswords—

namely, Farrar. After the 1920s success of the Simon & Schuster crossword series, which she continued to produce until 1978, she resigned from the *New York World*. Shortly thereafter she settled down with publisher John Farrar, co-founder of the esteemed publishing house that is now Farrar, Straus and Giroux. In addition to the crossword puzzle book series, Farrar was busily supplying puzzles for the armed forces publications. How fortunate for the acrossionado set that she accepted Sulzberger's challenge on the spot. With the First Lady of Crosswords on board, Sulzberger's next step was to revisit the newspaper's policy explicitly forbidding pencil games from sullying its pages.

To conform to the newspaper's lofty standards, the publisher and Farrar agreed that the puzzle ought to reflect newsworthy issues. This agreement introduced newsworthy names and places to the puzzle, distinguishing it from the dictionary-style newspaper crosswords. Under this guise, the *Times* management relented. Despite the mandate to reflect the issues of the day, because they were so dire, Farrar's main criterion for submissions was: "Good news preferred." Her three further requirements were (1) no two-letter words, (2) no diseases, and (3) nothing in bad taste. Initially, her job was to produce one page a week for the Sunday magazine, much as she had in her early days when the *New York World* presented its Word Cross in the Fun section.

Twenty years into her career, Farrar had a stable of regular constructors. In addition, she invited newcomers to test their puzzle prowess, including Sulzberger (who rose to the challenge). The weekly feature made its debut the day after Valentine's Day 1942. At the top of the page was the newsworthy puzzle, whimsically titled "Headlines and Footnotes" by Charles Erlenkotter, and "Riddle Me This," a puns-and-anagram-style crossword by the pseudonymous Anna Gram ran at the bottom part of the page. The Sunday puzzle-solving ritual was born on a national scale, and *Times* readers expected two puzzles for their money: one covering current events and another for diversion. This winning formula continues undisturbed to this day. Despite the double feature, the solving majority concentrates its skills on the top of the page and tosses out the one that is intended to divert. Just draw a line through every Sunday on the calendar as a day lost to puzzling, which is the way cartoonist Roz Chast looks at it.

Bad luck that the daily crossword, the modern compulsion that punctuates the day for tens of millions of puzzle folks, first appeared on a mid-September date in 1950 now branded forever in the annals of history—namely September 11.

━ ▭ ▭ ━

Erlenkotter produced a jumbo 23 × 23 for the debut puzzle in February 1942. Perhaps it burned him out because he merits only a single listing for his role as the first Sunday *Times* crossword constructor using Google to conduct an Internet search. Strange to look back at the old-fashioned punctuation of the clue list: Periods follow both numbers and clues, which read like sentences. Modern clue numbers appear in bold type with the only punctuation the occasional question mark at the end to indicate wordplay.

A review of the four-letter words from that puzzle reveals familiar repeaters. In the antique puzzle, **PEAR** answers to *puzzle clue:* "22. Obovoid pome." Contemporary crosswords prefer a descriptive synonym puzzle clue, such as "Bosc or Anjou." A term like *obovoid,* as in the shape of a female silhouette, has gone the way of the **REO** (*puzzle clue:* "Old-time motorcar"), which carries the monogram of auto manufacturer Ransom E. Olds (*E* for "Eli"). What a dry description for a sensuous fruit that inspired impressionist masterpieces by Cezanne. Yet **VELD** answers to *puzzle clue:* "133. Open country in Transvaal." This latter clue could qualify for use today, thanks to its reference to the country of origin. Then the constructor reverts to *Webster's* in his treatment of the Crosswordese verb **CITE**, with *puzzle clue:* "Adduce." How pleased Sulzberger must have been with such reporter speak.

Did Farrar filter out the hard-core four-letter words, those pesky repeaters that qualify as Crosswordese? With puzzle constructors advised to keep the clichés to a minimum, high marks go to the lady—only a baker's dozen appear in the Sunday debut crossword:

ACROSS		ANSWER
7.	Resourceful.	**ABLE**
73.	Lake of which Put-in-Bay is part.	**ERIE**
147.	Aggrieved.	**SORE**
148.	Indefinite quantity.	**DEAL**

DOWN		ANSWER
5.	Stead.	**LIEU**
10.	Hermes' son.	**EROS**
51.	Seaway.	**GATE**
52.	"What, never? Hardly —."	**EVER**
59.	Mouse-like rodent.	**VOLE**
60.	Poetical ideal of wifely devotion.	**ENID**
85.	Sterilizing apparatus.	**OVEN**
91.	Adduce.	**CITE**
92.	Pertaining to the armpit.	**ALAR**
131.	Aaron Burr's daughter.	**THEO**

Puzzle solvers recognize the four-letter words, despite the antiquated clues. Take the repeaters starting with **E**. Doesn't old standby **ERIE** sound fresh in the clue about Put-in-Bay, Ohio, population 128 (2000 census)? Each summer a million tourists flock to this village on South Bass Island to see the port where commander Oliver Hazard Perry waged his defense against the British in the War of 1812. Put-in-Bay also prides itself on offering fishermen one of the richest areas in the nation for bass, walleye, and perch. What a nice way to dress up this old chestnut.

Another **E** repeater, **EROS** (*puzzle clue:* "Greek god of love") makes its mark in modern clues as a Piccadilly landmark, my favorite in London. Dull adverb **EVER** now answers to the missing link in *puzzle clue:* "Happily — after." As for old **ENID**, the money is on *puzzle clue:* "Author Bagnold," the woman who penned *National Velvet* (1935) and provided Elizabeth Taylor with her first starring film role. In private life she was Lady Jones, wife of Sir Roderick, the chairman of Reuters news service. Sometimes she is disguised as "Author Bagnold of 'The Chalk Garden.'" That play became the film that launched Hayley Mills and co-starred her dad, Sir John, Deborah Kerr, and Dame Edith Evans (whose role garnered her a nomination for Best Supporting Actress). Known for her quips, the author said, "As for death, one gets used to it, even if it's only other people's you get used to." Bagnold dominates as the numero uno **ENID**, challenged only by the city in Oklahoma (*puzzle clue:* "Garfield county seat") voted one of the fifty top cities in the country.

Erlenkotter includes two perennial **A** repeaters in the grid.

Good old **ABLE** has held up over time. How often it fills in as a missing link in the palindrome *puzzle clue:* "— was I ere I saw Elba." (A palindrome is a phrase or word that reads the same from left to right and from right to left.) It is sometimes *puzzle clue:* "Suffix for do," or a straightforward synonym, as in this crossword. **ALAR**, used in its anatomical sense here, has reinvented itself as *puzzle clue:* "Banned apple spray." The pesticide was outlawed in 1989 when it was found to contaminate orchards. New definitions for four-letter words breathe new life into the old terms, especially when they make headlines, even when they're toxic.

A slangy clue yields a slangy answer to make sense in the Crossword lexicon. To my ear, *puzzle clue:* "Aggrieved" does not capture the gist of the four-letter word **SORE** as used by, say, Tony in HBO's *The Sopranos. Puzzle clue:* "Ticked off" or "Burned up" is more like it in the sense of irked. Rather than lab equipment, **OVEN** has turned into the familiar answer to *puzzle clue:* "Pizzeria fixture." Another clue that wouldn't ring a bell for today's puzzle solver is "Aaron Burr's daughter." Daddy's girl Theodosia (1783–1813), pet name **THEO**, was lost at sea en route from New York to South Carolina. An only child, she left poor Aaron crushed. After he iced Alexander Hamilton in the famous duel of 1805, our nation's third **VEEP** (*puzzle clue:* "#2") found solace in his one and only child. To the Eugene T. Maleska–era puzzle solver, **THEO** responds to *puzzle clue:*

"Vincent's brother," the art dealer who represented his brother Van Gogh. In recent years, the puzzle clue has become "Huxtable son," the character played by Malcolm-Jamal Warner on *The Cosby Show*. Theo Huxtable struggled with dyslexia, which could flummox a puzzle solver. The *Cosby* series was number one for five consecutive seasons, according to the Nielsen ratings, up there with — *in the Family* (**ALL**).

To spice up the four-letter roster, Farrar permits foreign ones in the debut crossword. As of *The Celebrities Cross Word Puzzle Book* (1925), she embraced Spanish words. At first, two-letter words were acceptable, specifically "Yes (Sp.)" for **SI**. By the 1940s, three letters became the minimum requirement. Puzzle creators, always chasing after new four-letter words, found a way to turn **SI** into a four-letter word. **SISI** now answers *puzzle clues:* "Spanish words of encouragement" and the appealing "Acapulco accord?" In crossword code, "Acapulco," the Pacific seaport, replaces the tag "(Sp.)." The *accord* in Acapulco indicates nothing more than vigorous agreement between two Spaniards. **HEHE**, as the answer goes to *puzzle clue:* "Giggle."

Three foreign-language repeaters appear in that debut Sunday puzzle:

"90. Mouth of a river (Sp.)." (**BOCA**). In the past sixty-five years this word has migrated to crossword geography as half of an American snowbird destination in Florida, known to all as *puzzle clue:* "— Raton."

"63. What Damon was to Pythias (Fr.)." (**AMI**). Quite modern in its presentation, although today's puzzle constructor prefers a French reference for a French word, as in *puzzle clue:* "Boyfriend, in Brest." Today, the four-letter **AMIE** has made itself equally at home in crosswords. As a rule, it answers to a puzzle clue such as "Valentine for Valery." In France, of course, Valéry is a man's name, as in ex-president Valéry Giscard d'Estaing.

"88. Of the (Fr.)." (**DES**). Boring clues like this one are **PASSE**, to use a five-letter repeater. Instead, this three-letter repeater is more often a missing link for *puzzle clue:* "— Moines."

"Headlines and Footnotes" also includes a smattering of four-letter words that fall into the dreaded realm of obsolete. If there is one other category crossword editors wrestle with after Crosswordese, it is contrived four-letter words like the **OHPT** nonsense that Roz Chast put in her revenge cartoon referred to in an earlier chapter. Solvers don't want to see endless repeaters, but neither do they want to pull out their hair in frustration at archaic terms. This crossword creaks in four instances.

"Egyptian goddess" (**APET**). Mount Olympus denizens provide diagram fodder more often than the deities from the Pyramids. Bring on **EROS** (*puzzle clue:* "Love god") and **HERA** (*puzzle clue:* "Zeus's consort") but keep your **APET** (aka Opet and Taueret), the mother of Osiris and a fertility goddess feted under Ramses II. Breaking the four-letters into two words, today's constructor would replace the clue as a missing link, as in *puzzle clue:* "In — (peeved)."

"Seaport of Honshu Island" (**HAGI**). A quaint castle town, this village is revered in Japan as the birthplace of political leaders of the mid-nineteenth century, such as its first modern prime minister, Ito Hirobumi (1841–1909), son of a samurai. Established circa 1600 during the **EDO** (*puzzle clue:* "Tokyo, once") era, Hagi has not changed much because public transportation has not yet reached it. Certainly, the village has faded from solving view in the last six decades. To make it more modern it could be redefined as the horticultural puzzle clue "Japanese bush clover."

"Geneva, in German" (**GENF**). Foreign words spice up the grid, it's true, but puzzle constructors favor Romance languages over German. Today's constructor would replace the final **F** in **GENF** to **X** for **GENX** (*puzzle clue:* "Boomers' babies") to describe those born between the 1960s and 1982. They are followed by **GENY**, folks born at the end of the twentieth century. The crop of babies born since 2000 are known as **GENZ**. After them, it's anyone's guess!

"Man's name" (**YVON**). Also banished are given names as answers with no external context. Granted, not many guys are called **YVON**! Only one comes to mind: "Patagonia founder Chouinard," founder of the all-weather-gear catalog. A former blacksmith, he set up the company in 1970 when he imported rugby shirts from Scotland. The shirts sold so well in Chouinard's native Maine that he developed a line of outdoor gear. Patagonia promotes environmental activism and even discontinued selling **PITONS** (*puzzle clue:* "Climber's aids") because they scar mountainsides. When Chouinard discovered how traditional cotton farms deplete the environment, he switched to pesticide-free organic cotton. Unfortunately, he was not available as a puzzle clue in 1942. The only **YVON** of that era is Jobin Yvon, the venerable manufacturer of optical equipment in Europe. In any case, the name has no place in Crosswordese, with its initial **Y**. Faced with reworking a corner of the grid with another **Y** name such as **YVES** (*puzzle clue:* "Actor Montand"), the solver can empathize with puzzle constructor Erlenkotter's decision to live with **YVON** and come up with a clue acceptable to Farrar.

■ ■ ■

The fact that Erlenkotter's byline never reappeared on the Sunday puzzle page speaks volumes. Whether he was a one-shot Sunday puzzle constructor or simply funneled his talents to the anonymity of the daily crossword, let's salute him for starting the Sunday *Times* puzzle tradition that shapes the day for Russell Baker and millions of puzzle solvers.

5

KEY FOUR-LETTER WORDS STARTING WITH E:
A Chain of Crossword E's

The most commonly used letters are
E, O, S, and M, in that order.

LAURA Z. HOBSON, BESTSELLING AUTHOR AND PUZZLE EDITOR

By the time I visited with Laura Z. Hobson, she had retired from her position as puzzle editor of *The Saturday Review* and was working on volume two of her autobiography. The first female executive at Time, Inc., and author of *Gentleman's Agreement* (1947), a number one bestseller immortalized on screen by "Actor Gregory" (**PECK**), Hobson stumbled into her puzzle career. She started out by constructing cryptograms (encoded messages) as a lark for the *Herald Tribune* at $1 **APOP** ("Each"). This exercise taught her the mechanics of four-letter words and their components. Then, in 1965, she was carping to the editor of *The Saturday Review*, her friend Norman Cousins, about the deterioration of its puzzle when he put her on the spot by naming her puzzle editor. In lieu of wages she accepted an unabridged dictionary, which looked as if it had served her well when she showed it to me twenty years later.

When the *New York World* launched the crossword in 1913, the approach was 100 percent *Webster's* dictionary. Readers enjoyed *puzzle clues:* "Fruit of the cedar" for **CONE** and "A passage for perspiration" for **PORE**. Humor was unintentional if you agree that *puzzle clue:* "What most men are" for **BALD** is worthy of a chuckle. Instead of Across and Down columns, all clues had two numbers. To find a word in the grid, the puzzle solver searched for both numbers: one coordinate for the starting box and one for the ending box. Four-letter words dominated in grids of fanciful proportions, never square but a dazzling assortment of arrows and zigzags. The Ur-diagram was diamond shaped with a diamond cutout in the center. Despite its exotic shape, the answers are hypnotically familiar. It is curious to find an old chestnut in the antique puzzle—namely, **NEVA** (*puzzle clue:* "A river in Russia"). This durable repeater made it into the crossword lexicon from day one!

The double-number clue system continued for the first ten years, when the crossword puzzle appeared exclusively in the

World. Even two-letter words were identified by two numbers. What a revelation when, in 1923, a puzzle fan—the mysterious "Radical"—dropped the editor a suggestion for reducing the clue to a single number. This new system required reorganizing the clue structure. Rather than using the modern Across and Down, in the early days editor Farrar sorted the clues as Horizontal and Vertical. By the 1940s, the friendlier terms Across and Down took over.

By the time the Simon & Schuster crossword collection made its splash in 1924, the grid had settled into the compact, iconic 15 × 15 black-and-white diagram that is universally recognized. The three editors of this collection recorded the series of fortunate events in "How the Crossword Craze Started, by the Starters," in a January 1925 issue of *Colliers.*

Thanks to the self-appointed Amateur Crossword Puzzle League of America, an anonymous document dated September 27, 1924, spells out the four basic rules for construction. All still apply except for the third rule:

1. The pattern shall interlock all over.
2. Only approximately one-sixth of the squares shall be black.
3. Only approximately 1/10 of the letters shall be *unkeyed* (i.e. read only in one direction).
4. The design shall be symmetrical.

Unkeyed in crosswords refers to isolated letters surrounded by black squares that belong to only one word. Modern American crosswords require that letters work in both directions. British crossword constructors, however, never adopted this rule, which makes it more difficult for American puzzle solvers to ace the other style of crossword. Having two approaches to a letter doubles the chances of the right result. In addition, the British clue system is composed of riddles, which often stump the average American solver. Curiously, the league disbanded immediately after setting out the rules, probably too preoccupied with puzzle solving to waste time on meetings.

■ ▭ ▭ ■

For decades, the dictionary game preoccupied American solvers. Its relationship to the dictionary gave the crossword the air of a classroom tool, with the puzzle solvers as scholars. Not that *Webster's* definitions are necessarily boring: Puzzle solver and Emmy-winning actress Michael Learned (star of TV's *The Waltons* and *Nurse*) once mentioned to me that solving with her son when he was in his formative years helped him understand the pleasures of reading and wordplay.

To prove Learned correct, what follows is a "word chain." A word chain is a spelling game from the I-spy generation that dates back to long car rides before auto manufacturers installed DVD players for backseat riders. Word-game players

like the challenge of connecting two words that
equal number of letters by changing one letter
move. To make the challenge greater, the starting and ending
words do not share any letters at all. For example, one possible
chain that connects **ARNOT** to **SOLVE** by changing one letter per move is this: **SOLVE** to **SALVE** to **HALVE** and so on
for another fifteen one-letter shifts before reaching **ARNOT**.
It has been done.

The word chain in this chapter strings together a series of
four-letter repeaters that could be subtitled "Running on **E**."
As Hobson notes at the beginning of this chapter, **E** is the
most commonly used letter in English. Put down that Black-
Berry and pick up a pencil. This series links the past to the
present—**ESSE** to **EBAY**—via repeaters and by changing one
letter at a time. Yes, the time has come to focus on the **ESSE**
(pronounced *ess-see*) of crosswords. If this four-letter word
means nothing to you at all, then congratulate yourself for getting this far in life without bumping into a Latin word that has
kept itself alive through the efforts of puzzle constructors. If
you recognize it as the answer to *puzzle clue:* "Existence: Lat."
or "To be, to Brutus," then you already have been introduced
to basic Crosswordese. Perhaps you have seen the phrase *Esse
quam videri* (To be rather than to seem) while visiting a university such as **DUKE** or **ELON** because this is the state motto
of North Carolina. Alternatively, you could be a graduate of

the esteemed Berklee College of Music up north, which also uses this motto. The phrase was lifted from Cicero's essay on friendship. Any connection between friendship and statehood or musicianship is moot, provided you can answer *puzzle clue:* "First word of North Carolina motto."

For the word-chain maven, you can get to **EBAY** in fewer steps. But to pack in the maximum number of repeaters, the following series takes a circuitous route. To be fluent in Crosswordese is to know a smattering of foreign four-letter words with a dash of archaic words thrown in for good measure.

Step 1: ESSE to ESNE (*ez-knee*)

The "Feudal worker" or "Anglo Saxon slave" (**ESNE**) continues as a career path only in clues. From the Old English word *asneis,* our laborer evokes harvest times during the reign of Athelstan, the warrior who kept the Vikings from invading England in the 900s. That other field hand of yore, **SERF** (from Latin *servus,* or "slave"), has a role in crosswords but not as a repeater. Words with **F** in last place are too awkward for frequent appearances.

Step 2: ESNE to ESTE (*ess-te*)

The missing link for "Villa d'—" (**ESTE**), a stately home outside of Rome, refers to the Italian noble family who built the place in the 1500s. Its terraced Tivoli Gardens include an amazing display of water features that spout, cascade, and splash and inspired Franz Liszt to compose a piece about them after he saw them. This Villa d'Este is not to be confused with the jet-setters' resort of the same name located on Lake Como. Maybe most solvers can't afford $1,000 per night, but we visit the place as often as puzzle constructors invite us. Same answer, alternate clue: "Ferrara family name."

Step 3: ESTE to ERTE (*air-tay*)

The answer to *puzzle clue:* "Designer for Lillian Gish" is **ERTE**. Born Romain de Tirtoff (1892–1990), this *fashionista* made his reputation as RT, pronounced à la français as *air-tay*. For more than two decades he contributed hundreds of covers to the fashion magazine *Harper's Bazaar* and created outrageous costumes for *Les Folies Bergere* in Paris. In 1988, at the age of ninety-five, he produced costumes for the Broadway musical *Stardust*. Only the grim reaper could force the man to retire. Although he may have faded from the public eye, he remains forever as a repeater.

Step 4: ERTE to ERNE (*urn*)

Hovering "Sea eagle" or the less-specific *puzzle clue:* "Marine flier" **ERNE** ranks as the number one crossword bird. Despite my Audubon membership, I have yet to spy this Greenland native, which is described as having a gray brown body and white tail. Chances are better that Athelstan of Olde England spotted the bird because the word derives from the English of his day. (Most annoying is the way it sometimes swoops in with its three-letter spelling of **ERN**.)

Step 5: ERNE to ERLE (*earl*)

From the dawn of the television era, crosswords derive one of the most popular boy's names by using an odd spelling of the name Earl (**ERLE**). Only one parent chose this unusual form for her son, who is the definitive "First name in court-room drama," the acclaimed author **ERLE** Stanley Gardner. His alter ego, Perry Mason, born in 1933, lives forever as actor Raymond **BURR** in television reruns. Remarkable to discover that Gardner was among the founding members of the Court of Last Resort (a precedent to Legal Aid), which reopened cases for those who may have been wrongly convicted. In the days before DNA analysis, these lawyers gave hope to death-row inmates. Kudos for **ERLE**! Despite many aliases (including A. A. Fair, Carleton Kendrake, and Charles J. Kenny), **ERLE** can give thanks that his mother's choice has survived the test of doing solving time.

Step 6: ERLE to ERIE

Hop on board! *Puzzle clue:* "Jay Gould railroad" (**ERIE**) never rests. Does a week ever go by without a stop at this Pennsylvania perennial? "Canal of song" or "Great Lake port," the answer is the same. After all, "I-90 runs along it." No matter that this is the fourth-largest city in its state or that it played a crucial role in defending the nation during the War of 1812. The word derives from a "Great Lake tribe" that settled on its southern shore. Technically an abbreviation of *Erielhonan*, **ERIE** is Iroquois for "long tail," a reference to the local mountain lion. The **ERIE** people spoke a form of Iroquois, despite the fact that the two tribes were mortal enemies. By 1700, an alliance of the Iroquois and Seneca conquered the **ERIE**, who ceased to exist—except in crosswords. Not to be confused with its five-letter Halloween related homonym, **EERIE** (*puzzle clue:* "Spooky").

Step 7: ERIE to ELIE

Replace the **R** with **L** to yield Nobel Peace Prize–winner **ELIE** Wiesel. Author of the bestselling memoir *Night*, the Holocaust survivor describes his harrowing experience as a young boy at Auschwitz. His immortality as "Author Wiesel" is guaranteed due to the unusual spelling of his first name (the more conventional version is **ELI**, as in "Actor Wallach"). Oprah featured Wiesel on her show; and, further cementing his name in the greater consciousness, he is under consideration as a candidate for the president of Israel. Romanian-born **ELIE** serves on the faculty at Boston University and has firmly supplanted his fellow repeaters who are removed by one letter: **ELIA** (*puzzle clue:* "Director Kazan") and blond bombshell **ELKE** (*puzzle clue:* "Actress Sommer," aka Mrs. Peter Sellers). Wiesel may soon be unseated by a sudden upsurge of popular women named **EDIE**, who answer to *puzzle clues:* "Sedgwick," "Falco," and "Britt on *Desperate Housewives.*"

Step 8: ELIE to ELEE

Thank you, "General Robert—" (**ELEE**), for retaining the middle initial (for Edward) in order to join the ranks of repeaters. Son of Henry Lee, a Revolutionary War hero (*puzzle clue:* "Winner at the Second Battle of Bull Run"), the Civil War military leader rallied the Confederates and remains forever the epitome of an American soldier. He married a descendant of Martha Washington and had a large family: three sons and four daughters.

Step 9: ELEE to ELLE (*ell*)

Make it a double **L** in the middle and we land in the pages of *People* magazine. Who has not admired lissome supermodel **ELLE** Macpherson? Like the author **SHEL** (Shelby Silverstein), **ELLE** is known in crosswords by the first syllable of her full given name, Eleanor. Before she made a splash in the swimsuit issue of *Sports Illustrated*, the standard clue for her nickname was "French pronoun" because technically it translates as "she." Perfect symmetry is the fact that a third clue for the word, "French fashion magazine," describes the publication that gave the Aussie beauty her big break. It is one vowel removed from top repeater **ELLA** (*puzzle clue:* "Singer Fitzgerald") and repeater-in-training **ELLO** (*puzzle clue:* "Cockney greeting"). Dropping the aitches gives puzzle constructors fresh opportunity for forging four-letter words like **ENRY** (*puzzle clue:* "Professor 'Iggins").

Step 10: ELLE to ELSE

Tough word among repeaters is the answer to missing-word *puzzle clue:* "Or —!" (**ELSE**). Sometimes it is simply the answer to *puzzle clue:* "Ultimatum word." Everyone who has ever threatened or been threatened can fill in that blank. Less threatening is the query that prompts the reply, "Just the check, please," meaning "Anything —?" It is one letter removed from the star of one of my favorite childhood films: **ELSA**. No, I am not referring to "Actress Lanchester," the wife of actor Charles Laughton and star of *The Bride of Frankenstein* (1935). My pet favorite is the *Born Free* (1966) lioness. Who can read the clue without humming the memorable theme song from the scene in which the lioness is forced to grow up and leave the bosom of her human family?

Step 11: ELSE to ERSE (*ers*)

Reintroduce **S** in the third square for the answer to *puzzle clue:* "Gaelic" (**ERSE**), the language of Ireland. For crossword solvers, the top four-letter foreign language is **ERSE**, an elision of the native tongue of the Irish, originally spelled as Eirish. Even its homonym, the three-letter **ERS** (*Ervum ervilia*; and *puzzle clue:* "Bitter vetch"), grows like Topsy in the grid. The language of the Celts plays an outsize role in Crosswordese, beginning with the synonyms for the Emerald Isle, such as the familiar **EIRE**. Keep the slogan "— go bragh" (**ERIN**) in mind for St. Patty's Day. And hats off to Julia Roberts, who has added an updated clue to repeaterdom with her star turn as "— Brockovich" in the film based on the story of **ERIN**, a trailer park mom who becomes an environmental activist and strikes it rich. Stay tuned for tricky *puzzle clue:* "Literally 'West Isle,'" referring to Ireland's position vis-à-vis Scotland.

Step 12: ERSE to ERST

Puzzle clue: "Once, once" (**ERST**) is the clever cross-eyed way of dressing up this archaic repeater, more familiar to Athelstan than to the modern eye. This type of trickery is what Roz Chast is lampooning in her cartoon of the nonsensical crossword. Although *erstwhile* has remained in common usage, the prefix meaning "formerly" no longer has a place in conversation. When have you done your erst? It brings to mind the adjective *ruthless*, meaning "without compassion." *Ruthful*, which was a valid word until Shakespeare's time, has gone the way of **ERST**. What the world needs now is more ruth, not less.

Step 13: ERST to ERAT

Attention, geometry experts and lawyers: Are you familiar with the three letters QED? No, not the prankster's version, "Quite easily done." The Latin phrase *Quod erat demonstratum* means "what was to be proven." It marks the conclusion of an argument. For crossword purposes, *puzzle clue:* "Part of QED" always refers to the four-letter word in the middle (**ERAT**). A **Q** word as a repeater? Not yet proven.

Step 14: ERAT to ETAT

Parlez-vous Crosswordese? The French repeater **ETAT** will serve the puzzle solver well. In the gentle days of yore, when crosswords were a dictionary-style game, constructors spoon-fed solvers the straightforward *puzzle clue:* "State: Fr." The language of origin was included as part of the clue. Nowadays, this particular repeater appears as *puzzle clue:* "French political division" or as the missing link "Coup d'—." Overthrow of the government by a small group of people in power—coup d'**ETAT** (literally, "blow to the state")—is a front-page item, and the term appears in English-language headlines. The other four-letter part of the term, *coup*, is not a repeater. Its two consonants are not the easiest to interlock, and **U** is also the least popular of the vowels.

Step 15: ETAT to ETAL

Puzzle clue: "List ending abbr." or "Series ender" (**ETAL**) is technically Latin, but anyone who has written a paper in school has had occasion to use it. Meaning "and others," that final **AL** is an abbreviation for two possible words: the masculine plural **ALII** and, more often, the neuter plural **ALIA**. There was a short span of puzzle time when **ALIA** answered *puzzle clue:* "Jordanian airline," but it has reverted to the missing link, as in "Et —." To determine whether the final letter is **A** or **I**, try to solve for the intersecting word.

Step 16: ETAL to ELAL

There is only one four-letter airline, and it flies from Tel Aviv—Ben Gurion International, to be exact. Since 1948, **ELAL** (translation: "skyward") has served as the flagship airline of Israel and is considered among the most secure airlines in the world, in addition to Hebrew's greatest contribution to Crosswordese.

Step 17: ELAL to EGAL

Why, oh why, do I love Paris? Because so many repeaters derive from there. Shades of *"Liberté, Égalité, Fraternité,"* the motto of the French republic! Instead of the French tag, as we saw in Step 14, the hint of the language of origin is implied by a mention of a French city or name with some alliteration for good measure as in *puzzle clue:* "Equal, in Evian" or "Even, to Yvette" (**EGAL**).

Step 18: EGAL to EGAD

Gadzooks, *puzzle clue:* "Mild expletive," "Yikes," or "Holy Toledo" (**EGAD**) to Oscar Wilde, who uses it in *The Picture of Dorian Gray.* The elision of *oh + God* yields an inoffensive exclamation that harks back to the seventeenth century. It sometimes appears in the plural as **EGADS**.

Step 19: EGAD to EGAN

Smart move for B-movie actor Richard **EGAN** to alter the spelling of his name from Eagan to the four-letter repeater, thus becoming immortalized as *puzzle clue:* "Richard of old Westerns." He may soon be unseated by "Carlton of the N.Y. Cardinals," a team that deserves some free publicity.

Step 20: EGAN to ELAN

Technically, the adjective **ELAN** is French, but has it been co-opted? It derives from the French verb that means to "throw a lance." How did the hurling of the lance make the leap to an adjective that describes *puzzle clue:* "Ardor"? Flair, liveliness, and panache all add up to that *je ne sais quoi.* The evolution of **ELAN** eludes me.

Step 21: ELAN to EBAN

Puzzle clue: "Statesman Abba" or "Israeli statesman" (**EBAN**), the diplomat was born Aubrey Solomon in South Africa in 1915. Educated at Cambridge, where he studied Middle Eastern languages, he served in the British army during World War II. In 1947 he was appointed to the United Nations committee that divided Palestine into separate Jewish and Arab states. As a result of his role in the birth of Israel, he assumed a Hebrew name (*abba* means "father") and became immortalized thanks to his four-letter first and last names.

Step 22: EBAN to EBAY

What a debt of gratitude puzzles owe to the Internet, opening up a world of new repeaters and redefining boring four-letter words like **SITE**. *Puzzle clue:* "It may do your bidding," "Big dot-com headquartered in San Jose," or "Silent auction site" (**EBAY**)—you know the place. World-renowned **EBAY**, originally "Echo Bay," was the brainchild of computer genius Pierre Omidyar. Someone else had already registered as Echo Bay before he got around to it, so Omidyar renamed his domain with the familiar four-letter term. **EBAY** launched in

1995 and made Omidyar a billionaire three years later when it went public.

The first item ever sold via the site was a broken laser pointer, to a collector of broken laser pointers. The buyer wanted only the broken ones. As puzzle solvers know, it takes all kinds—of four-letter words, that is.

6

AROUND THE WORLD IN FOUR-LETTER WORDS:
Armchair Traveling

Start with what you know and build on it.

BILL CLINTON, FORTY-SECOND PRESIDENT OF
THE UNITED STATES AND PUZZLE SOLVER

Thanks to President Clinton for the advice he offers in the documentary *Wordplay*. That's the sort of crossword insight that acrossionados like to share, but may I point out he is building on a broader base of knowledge than most of us. Foreign-language four-letter words, in particular, can be Greek to the notoriously provincial American solver. To quote Gus from the film *My Big Fat Greek Wedding*, it does sometimes feel as if many words were derived from Greek. The land of Mount **OSSA** (*puzzle clue:* "Peak in Thessaly") contributes three rhyming four-letter words: **BETA** (*puzzle clue:* "Phi — Kappa"),

FETA (*puzzle clue:* "Greek salad topper"), and **ZETA** (*puzzle clue:* "Epsilon follower"), the latter now vying with movie star "Catherine — Jones." Greek's most popular letters are vowels **ETA** and **IOTA**. The former has morphed into *puzzle clue:* "Airport abbr." to mean a short version of *estimated time of arrival.* Although it is the ninth letter in the Greek alphabet, in crosswords **IOTA** translates to a smidgen, as in these *puzzle clues:* "Tiniest bit," "Jot," and "Shred."

Currency is where puzzle solvers seem most comfortable. In modern Europe, including Greece, *puzzle clue:* "Continental coin" is the newly minted four-letter, vowel-heavy **EURO**. It ousted the German **MARK**; but, luckily for puzzle constructors, the **PESO** survives as *puzzle clue:* "Mexican money" or "Coin in Cancún." (Alliteration is favored in the spirit of wordplay when possible, as I keep hammering on about.) Puzzle constructors serve up *puzzle clue:* "Old Italian bread" for the centuries-old **LIRA**, using the synonym for "dough" or "money." All in an effort to tease and amuse puzzle solvers.

Geography-wise, most puzzle solvers are clear on the states that **ABUT** (*puzzle clue:* "Border") their home state. For example, **SDAK** abuts **NDAK**. Travel farther afield and which country is where starts getting fuzzy. Four-letter words on the crossword map consist mainly of bodies of water and disproportionately emphasize islands, particularly Hawaii and Ireland. Add in a string of vowel-rich world capitals, and off you go.

For me, crossword geography goes back to the history lesson embodied by *puzzle clue:* "Capital of La Manche," the area of Normandy that abuts the English Channel—namely **STLO**. Forever "World War II town" in puzzle clues, it symbolizes the **DDAY** campaign (*puzzle clue:* "June 6, 1944" or "Do or die time"), or the Allied offensive on the shores of Normandy that ended with the liberation of Paris. One of the quirks of crossword culture is how it seems to thrive in wartime: It was born on the eve of World War I and, after a slump, regained popularity during World War II. Do solvers appreciate how the four-letter answer to *puzzle clue:* "June 6, 1944" embodies the valiant 29th Infantry Division who helped wrest France from its four years in the clutches of the Axis nations? From the port of Plymouth, England, Allied soldiers crossed the Channel to land in **STLO**, a town of twenty thousand, and changed the course of history. Almost entirely destroyed in battle, the city was called the "Capital of the Ruins" by Samuel Beckett. Even if solvers do not pause to reflect on its role in history, they will forever bump into this useful repeater, which combines three consecutive common consonants and ends in **O**. Puzzle constructors try to trick puzzle solvers with the other "D-Day town" for **CAEN**, or "Capital of Lower Normandy." Separated from **STLO** by only a few miles, **CAEN** was first sacked in 1346 by Edward III of England and then overlooked for six hundred years. Its claim to fame is that William the Conqueror is buried there. Each town is situated on a four-letter river: **STLO** on the Vire, and **CAEN** on the Orne—yet neither river has made it to repeatersville.

Crosswords almost blew the cover off the secrecy surrounding this crucial military maneuver in an unnerving sequence of events in the weeks preceding the D-Day invasion. Coincidence or sabotage? Historians are still trying to solve the puzzle of how the *Daily Telegraph* crossword sparked the "panic of 1944." During May of that year, the crossword grabbed the attention of British MI5 officials, and on the sixtieth anniversary of D-Day, journalists were still speculating about how particular four-letter words emerged in six puzzles just as troops were mobilizing. Generals Eisenhower and Montgomery kept the dates of the attack top secret, even shifting from June 5 to June 6 due to weather conditions. Their communiqués were in code known only to insiders. Yet right up to the actual event, select four-letter words popped up in the *Daily Telegraph*. Was someone on the inside trying to tip off a German spy solver about what was about to happen?

The first puzzle to arouse suspicion appeared in the May 3 edition of the *Telegraph*. What piqued the interest of the puzzle solvers of the Military Intelligence group known as MI5 was the four-letter word **UTAH**. This southwest state was code for the D-Day beach assigned to the U.S. 4th Assault Division. Benignly, it answered *puzzle clue:* "One of the USA (4)." (British puzzles provide the number of letters in the answer parenthetically.) To distract themselves during hours spent in air-raid shelters during the blitzkrieg, the British turned to the puzzle page, and intelligence officers were no exception. **UTAH** caught their attention and created a buzz among those in the know. In quick succession, the puzzle included two other four-letter words with double meanings: **JUNO** and **GOLD**. Hullo! Not just innocent answers to *puzzle clues:* "Roman goddess" and "Precious metal," these were the code names for the beaches assigned to the British forces. Four-letter words do tend to repeat, but this was worrying.

Official solvers kept close tabs on the puzzle. On May 22, they were jolted by a five-letter word for *puzzle clue:* "Red Indian on the Missouri (5)." The answer **OMAHA** is now known to have been the code word for the Normandy beaches. Five days later, "Big-wig (8)" clued for the unusual answer **OVERLORD**, code word for the whole operation. On May 30, MI5 officials were horrified to see **MULBERRY**, the secret word for the floating harbors that the Allies planned to move across the Channel to keep their supply boats in fuel. Finally, just five days before the invasion, the answer to 15 Down was **NEPTUNE**, which was code for the key naval offensive.

Shades of **DIEPPE**, another northern French town along the Bay of the Seine! Two summers earlier, the crossword had come under scrutiny for possible espionage before a similar invasion. An intelligence officer by the colorful name of Lord Tweedsmuir noted that **DIEPPE** appeared in the puzzle on August 17; the solution was published on August 18, the eve of the invasion of that town in Normandy. Was this a puzzle constructor's cunning plan to pass along classified information? After some investigation, Tweedsmuir dismissed his suspicions as the result of an overheated imagination. But that was just a single clue: In May 1944, there was a whole series, which added up to the big push.

A pair of officers paid a visit to Leatherhead, Surrey, to interrogate Leonard Dawe, the compiler (Brit-speak for "puzzle constructor") and head of Strand, a boys' school. The school was temporarily evacuated to the suburbs from London to keep the boys out of the way of the bombs. Understandably, Dawe was horrified to be suspected of treason. As is typical among academics, Dawe supplemented his income by dabbling in the crossword field. Why these particular words? He pointed out there is no law against using them. True, but not a satisfactory explanation, which prompted the officers to seek out his fellow compiler, Melville Jones. After much discussion, the officials concluded it was an amazing coincidence.

Years later, the BBC interviewed Dawe about the incident. He recalled being "turned inside out" during the grilling. Evidently, puzzles have a certain hold over world events! Conspiracy theorists, never content to leave well enough alone, revisit the subject on each decade anniversary of D-Day. Over the years, several "old boys," as alumni are called, have explained how it came about. In 1984 Ronald French broke a vow of silence after four decades. In his version, Dawe often selected top students to help with puzzle constructing, which he considered "an excellent mental discipline." At age fourteen, French had been among the younger assistants. After school, he spent much of his free time with the troops camped nearby. The D-Day invasion was rehearsed for months before the actual event, so the boy heard the soldiers' conversations. Code words were openly used; the only secret was when it would take place. French offered the overheard words to the headmaster. After the MI5 investigators left, French recalled, the headmaster spoke to him about a diary that the boy filled with overheard tidbits. The book was promptly burned, and the boy sworn to secrecy.

Another version of the story arose in 2004. Strand graduate Richard S. J. Wallington confirmed that Dawe asked older boys for help when compiling puzzles. With loudmouth American troops in the area, the boys were privy to what turned out to be classified information, which they passed along and got the old man in hot water, possibly as a prank.

▪ ▪ ▪ ▪

Crossword rivers span in a network from England across to Russia. Alphabetically, the route zigzags on its course from west to east. Solvers anticipate the two top **A** rivers: **AARE** and **AIRE**. Excellent double **A** in the first position for four-letter **AARE**, which connects two scenic lakes, Neuchatel and Thun. This durable repeater from Switzerland (*puzzle clue:* "River of Bern") flows in the western part of the country. Not to be confused with the English river removed by one letter, the homonym for the stuff we inhale: **AIRE**. In the northern reaches, it is the "West Yorkshire river" that answers to *puzzle clue:* "River of Leeds." Travel to the northernmost tip of Northumberland to find another top repeater, *puzzle clue:* "Newcastle-upon- —" (**TYNE**). Also answer to these clues: "Newcastle river" and "— and Wear," it dominates the rugged landscape of the industrial area south of the Cheviot Hills of Scotland. Beware the homonym that answers to *puzzle clue:* "Fork prong" (**TINE**).

England is awash in repeater rivers. Best known is *puzzle clue:* "The Bard's river" (**AVON**). How gratifying to fill it in a missing-link clue, "Stratford-upon- —." To ramp up the challenge, the alternative is *puzzle clue:* "River to the Severn." The Severn flows through Gloucestershire and the scenic Cotswold Hills southward into the Bristol Channel. Of course, **AVON** is more than a river: It is the county for both Bristol and Bath. And locally in the United States it answers to a brand of makeup as in the saleslady who rings the doorbell (*puzzle clue:* "— calling").

Traveling to Norfolk on the northeastern shore of England, how thrilling to ford the familiar **OUSE** (*puzzle clue:* "River of NE England" or "River to The Wash"). Technically, it connects the town of King's Lynn on a North Sea inlet called The Wash to St. **IVES** (alternative *puzzle clue:* "Actor Burl" as well as "St. —, Cornwall resort") in Cambridgeshire. As puzzle solvers know, London's East End plays a big role in crosswords, which gives this river the option of masquerading as "Cockney residence." ("Cockney" is code for dropping the initial **H**.) This Norfolk waterway is not to be confused with a river separated by one vowel, **OISE**, which is most often the answer to the opaque *puzzle clue:* "French river." Tucked by the border of Belgium, this river flows through an eponymous region and into a Parisian suburb, "Val d'—" (**OISE**). Versatile river it is, answering to three *puzzle clues:* "River of Chantilly," "Seine feeder," and "Ardennes river."

Germany boasts two top repeater rivers: **EDER** and **ODER**. The former is "River of Hesse," the western German region of which Frankfurt is capital. The other, or should I say the **ODER**, flows along the border of eastern Germany and becomes the **ODRA** in Poland. Traveling farther east is another pair of rivers with girlish names: **LENA** and **NEVA**. The perennial *puzzle clue:* "Singer Horne" finally has competition from the meandering "Siberian river" that joins the Arctic Ocean to inland

Russia. Ports along the way include Yakutsk and Lensk, which sometimes make a cameo as a reference in the clue.

Russia also contributes two winning repeaters separated by the first vowel. One is a sea, the other most often a mountain range, ending in – **RAL**. Start with an **A** to reach *puzzle clue:* "Asia's landlocked — Sea" (**ARAL**). In the southern Kazakh region of Russia, made infamous by the Sasha Baron Cohen film *Borat*, the sea gets footage in Pulitzer Prize–winner Al Gore's documentary *An Inconvenient Truth*. The level of the **ARAL** is noticeably diminishing as it seems to be drying up. Global warming is one factor, and unwise irrigation techniques have been proven to be another. Bad news for folks in nearby Aral'sk and Kazalinsk. Traveling west through Kazakh you hit the dual-purpose **URAL**. As a river, you find *puzzle clue:* "Orsk is on it"; but it also answers to *puzzle clue:* "Russian mountain range." Orsk has great potential to overtake the repeater *puzzle clue:* "Approximately" for **ORSO**. That final **K** is a mixed blessing.

Most popular repeater river the **YSER** is located in Belgium. Each letter is so versatile that you predictably run into this river weekly. The answer to *puzzle clue:* "It flows in Flanders" or "Nieuwpoort's river," it is an unassuming waterway on the border of France by the North Sea. Not to be confused with the five-letter homonym repeater **ISERE**, which flows through Grenoble in the south of France. The two rivers are pronounced in the same way, so they're easy to confuse. My personal favorite four-letter river is a homonym for my surname: "Florence is on it" (**ARNO**). Italy rounds out its contribution to Crosswordese with two more repeaters: a volcano and a city. *Puzzle clue:* "Sicilian spouter" and "Noted Tower site" yield **ETNA** and **PISA**, respectively. Call it "Birthplace of Galileo" or "Fermi university town," it all adds up to the place with the leaning tower.

■ ▪ ▫ ▫

Back on home turf, the two states that enrich Crosswordese are the ones farthest from the mainland. Hawaii is particularly rich in repeaters, thanks to the placement of **U** and **I** in native four-letter words. At the top of the heap are *puzzle clues:* "Hawaiian cookout" (**LUAU**); "Luau lamp" (**TIKI**); and "Hawaiian dance" (**HULA**), which has an alternate missing-link *puzzle clue:* "— hoop." Hot vacation destinations include *puzzle clues:* "Pearl City setting" or "Waikiki locale" (**OAHU**), "Hawaiian port" (**HILO**), and "Hawaiian isle" (**MAUI**). Thanks to Starbucks, we all know coffee is a crop of *puzzle clue:* "Hawaiian coastal area" (**KONA**). What goes with **JAVA** (*puzzle clue:* "Diner cuppa")? *Puzzle clue:* "Poi source" (**TARO**) fills the bill. **TARO** is a potato's cousin (aka *corm*); and although it is eaten widely, only Hawaiians pound it to a pulp and eat it off their fingers. Haloa, the sacred Hawaiian spirit, resides in each bowl of poi and keeps the peace at the dining table. Change the menu with the "Hawaiian dish" **PELE**, now that the soccer great who answers to that name has faded from sight. As for the state bird? Puzzlers know it is the **NENE**, or black-faced Hawaiian goose. Despite all these popular four-letter words, the key Hawaiian repeater counts only three letters: "Hawaiian neckwear" (**LEI**).

A stopover in the Aleutian Islands by the North Pole in the Bering Sea reveals two top repeaters. **ATTU** belongs to the far west subdivision called the Near Islands, whereas **ATKA** is to the far east among the Andreanof Islands. It seems appropriate that names of small land masses fit so well in the puzzle grid. The predominant one, as mentioned in the chain of four-letter words explored in Chapter 5, is **ERIN** or **EIRE**, *puzzle clue:* "The Emerald Isle," where **ERSE** (*puzzle clue:* "Gaelic") is spoken. Solvers are familiar with *puzzle clue:* "Galway Bay islands" (**ARAN**), source of the famous jumper (sweater) knitted from natural yarn and often called "the fisherman's sweater." Turning the tables, **ISLE** itself answers to tricky *puzzle clue:* "Man, for one," a reference to an island in the Irish Sea, where it meets the North Channel, rather than the male of the species.

The Spanish version, **ISLA**, is making inroads, answering to *puzzle clue:* "Ibiza, e.g." (To keep clues short, puzzle constructors opt for "e.g." [for example] and "i.e." [that is].) When in Mexico, you can visit *puzzle clue:* "— Mujeres." **ISLA** also serves as the given name of a co-star of *Scooby-Doo* (2002) and *Wedding Crashers* (2005) and *puzzle clue:* "Actress Lang Fisher."

Geographical repeaters rely on a riff of four-letter words that start with **O**. In ascending order of appearance, there is an airport and a state plus an **OLIO** (*puzzle clue:* "Hodgepodge") of cities. You might transit *puzzle clue:* "Paris airport" (**ORLY**) to reach "Nobel city" (**OSLO**), the capital of Norway. Change the second syllable for "Peak in Thessaly" (**OSSA**), with its enviable position on the Aegean coast of Greece. Don't be fooled by tricky *puzzle clue:* "Athens setting," which has nothing to do with Greece but refers to the vowel-rich state of **OHIO**. Athens is a county in the southeast of the state that borders on West Virginia. Traveling west, Utah town **OREM** is gaining popularity, described variously as "City east of Utah Lake," "North of Provo," and "Next to Uinta Forest."

On the other side of the world, a sliver of a country nestled beside Saudi Arabia on the Arabian Sea has proven itself a stalwart repeater. *Puzzle clue:* "Sultanate" or "Gulf War ally" refers to **OMAN**. Replace **O** with **I** for "Single-named supermodel" or "Mrs. David Bowie" (**IMAN**), also an eponymous brand of cosmetics. Shift the first consonant to **R** for **ORAN** (*puzzle clue:* "Camus' birthplace") on the coast of Algeria, or "'The Plague' setting," referring to the novel by Albert Camus. With Camus's brand of existentialism no longer in fashion, I treasure my copy of *The Myth of Sisyphus.* As Camus retells the ancient tale of the "absurd hero" condemned to a life of pushing a boulder up a hill only to watch it roll back down, "his passion for life won him that unspeakable penalty in which the whole being is exerted toward accomplishing nothing." No matter how he labors, good old Sisyphus returns to square one. The philosopher sees this act as symbolic of life's daily struggle, with the rock becoming the main focus. I imagine that this allegory also describes the life of a solver: No sooner do you complete one puzzle than you are faced with tackling the next one. "The struggle towards the heights is enough to fill a man's heart," writes Camus. Same goes for puzzles. You can't let moss grow under your feet with crosswords: Keep your bags packed, because the journey never ends.

■ ■ ■

Now is the moment to shut *Webster's Unabridged* (or log off www.dictionary.com) and consider four-letter words with an accent. I believe you will be pleasantly surprised at how many you already know. If you ever tackled a Mexican **TACO** (*puzzle clue:* "South of the border order") or sipped French "Café au —" (**LAIT**), you already have a head start on two repeaters. And

MERCI ("Thanks, in Toulouse") to Starbucks for minting two tasty new foreign-language repeaters to go: The Italian word for milk (**LATTE**), has turned into familiar *puzzle clue:* "Tall coffee order" and tea in Chinese (**CHAI**) is now the answer to *puzzle clue:* "Starbucks option."

Crossing the Pond, as the British describe the Atlantic, the grand tour of repeaters begins at *puzzle clue:* "London gallery" or "Gallery showing Turner" (**TATE**). The East End dialect is a neat excuse to whittle down five-letter words into four. *My Fair Lady* is the touchstone for **H**-free Cockney as *puzzle clue:* "Professor 'Iggins" (Eliza's mentor) becomes **ENRY**. The term for this accent is derived from "cock's egg," for reasons known better to Shakespeare. Take the 'int and solve h'accordingly, mate. *Puzzle clue:* "Cockney greeting" becomes **ELLO** and "Lends a 'and" yields **ELPS**, no initial apostrophe to replace the missing **H**. (Apostrophes have no job in the grid.)

The East End also contributes a useful three-letter repeater to the lexicon: **LOO** (*puzzle clue:* "W.C.," for water closet). The British euphemism for toilet derives from the French four-letter word **LIEU** (place). After downing *puzzle clue:* "Pub order" (**PINT**) ask for the "Gents, e.g." or "Ladies, e.g." and you will end up in the **LOO**.

Spanish and French are rich sources of four-letter words. Each supply commonly known answers that conveniently end in **A** or **O**. Four-letter words that appear often in Crosswordese include useful four-letter words such as **HOLA** (*puzzle clue:* "Spanish greeting") and **ESTA** (*puzzle clue:* "Spanish pronoun"), often filling in the blank for "Como — usted?" (How are you?). Perennial *puzzle clues:* "Madrid Mrs." (**SRA**) and "Madrid Ms." (**SRTA**) eclipse their male equivalent, **SENOR**. An abbreviation in a clue indicates a shortened answer, as I've mentioned elsewhere, so don't wonder at how to squeeze **SENORITA** into four boxes. Honorifics **DON** and **DONA** fill in the missing links for the Cervantes classic "— Quixote" and a Brazilian film with a brilliant career as a clue, "— Flor and Her Two Husbands."

Most popular members of the Spanish family unit are female, led by the aunt, **TIA**, aka "— María." **NINA**, the generic "Spanish girl," has the option of masquerading as "One of Columbus's ships" or "One of a sailboat trio" with the *Pinta* and *Santa María* out of the running. Legendary caricaturist Al Hirschfeld celebrated his only child, Nina, by disguising the letters of her name in his sketches. By adding her name into the images, his drawings became visual puzzles. The number of times the name *Nina* appears per sketch is indicated by the number placed by his signature. The challenge of finding them all has become a standardized test required by the U.S. government to test pilots training for combat! For seventy years, until he passed away at age one hundred in 2003, Hirschfeld amused readers of the *New York Times* Arts and Leisure section with this game. Other **NINA**s of note include *puzzle clue:* "Folksinger Simone" or "Socialite Griscom." (Attention, aspiring rock stars: This name is up for grabs in crossword clues.)

Proceed to *puzzle clue:* "Spanish residence" (**CASA**), sometimes described as: "Latin quarters?" (Quarters in the sense of a residence, not coins.) Enter the **SALA** (room) where you might awaken *puzzle clue:* "Mouse catcher in Madrid" (**GATO**). At the doorway you pass an **OLLA** (*puzzle clue:* "Earthenware jar"). **OLLA** is also the answer to the missing word in: "— podrida" *Olla podrida*, literally "powerful stew," is a traditional Spanish dish made from red beans, chorizo, and other spicy ingredients cooked in a clay pot. Sancho Panza rhapsodizes on the hearty stew in *Don Quixote*. In its Anglicized form, **OLLA** becomes the crossword cliché **OLIO**, which, as mentioned earlier, means a literal stew or mixture.

The Spanish sport with crossword legs generates from the *corrida*, where the main attraction is *puzzle clue:* "Matador's opponent" (**TORO**). Sans **O**, **TOR** is the repeater "Rocky peak." Add **A** for *puzzle clue:* "When said three times, WWII film" (**TORA! TORA! TORA!**), a film that chronicles the Japanese attack on Pearl Harbor. *Tora*, Japanese for tiger, was the code word for the attack. Shifting the final vowel, there's **TORE** ("Made tracks") and **TORI** ("Famous Amos"), the rock-and-roll singer born Myra Ellen. The cheer that echoes through puzzles is **OLE**. Wave **ADIOS** (*puzzle clue:* "Goodbye, in Granada" or Guadalajara—your choice)!

■ ■ ■

ALLO (*puzzle clue:* "French greeting")! Puzzle solvers transit *puzzle clue:* "Airport in Paris" (**ORLY**) flying over "— de la Cite" or "Isle: Fr." (**ILE**). No worries about the articles *le* and *la* in crossword French, since they are nonexistent for puzzle people. *Puzzle clue:* "— bien!" (**TRES**) is "very good!" At "Night, in Nantes" (**NUIT**), the puzzle solver sips "Pinot —" (**NOIR**) with **PATE** or **BRIE** (*puzzle clues:* "French spread" and "French cheese," respectively). In a bistro you order "— carte" or pie "— mode" (**ALA**) in three consecutive boxes with no space between the words. Because states are now abbreviated to two letters, and crosswords require three letters, constructors have moved on from calling **ALA** *puzzle clue:* "Neighbor of Fla."

Frenchmen are said to be ruled by the **TETE** (*puzzle clue:* "French head"). They ponder the "Raison d'—" (**ETRE**) of life, which also answers *puzzle clue:* "To be, in Toulouse." So much emphasis on thinking explains the puzzle power of top repeater **IDEE** (*puzzle clue:* "French notion" or the clever "Brainstorm in Paris"). It turns into a full-blown passion in the phrase "— fixe," meaning "obsession." Despite its puzzle-unfriendly letters, *fixe* also follows **PRIX**, as in "— fixe" for a "fixed price" set menu or early-bird special.

A young woman in Paris is **MLLE** (short for Mademoiselle), as in **GIGI**, *puzzle clues:* "Colette heroine" and "Leslie Caron role," referring to the 1958 film. Tussaud is a well-known **MME** (Madame). Parisian parents are called **PERE** and **MERE**. Once upon a time, the nineteenth-century Honoré de Balzac novel "— Goriot" was the standard missing-link clue for **PERE**. The only month that counts is **AOUT** (August) during the high season in crossword French, which is summer, or **ETE**. *Puzzle clue:* "Nice season," is understood to be the upper-case Nice, the Riviera port. Of course, summer is also a nice season. "Sacre —" (**BLEU**), to borrow a mild oath from *Gigi*.

■ ▪ ■

ACH (*puzzle clue:* "German expression") In my early days as a puzzle solver, crosswords taught me the nickname for West German chancellor Konrad Adenauer. It was the four-letter **ALTE**, missing link to *puzzle clue:* "Der —." The phrase trans-lates as "the old man," and Adenauer earned the endearment by staying in office until the age of eighty-seven. Puzzle con-structors now replace the final vowel for *puzzle clue:* "Choir member" (**ALTO**). Sorry, Chancellor Adenauer, you are truly history. Most useful German four-letter word in the twenty-first century is the article **EINE**, and Mozart supplies the missing-link *puzzle clue:* "— Kleine Nachtmusik" ("A Little Night Music"). An alternative puzzle clue is "Single, in Stuttgart." The only Teutonic number that counts in puzzles is **DREI**, which answers to the dry puzzle question: "German crowd?" Finally, **NEIN** (*puzzle clue:* "Opposite of ja," aka "Ruhr refusal") evokes the river that runs through Essen and into the Rhine.

The word from Moscow is short and sweet, *puzzle clue:* "Russian refusal" (**NYET**).

* * *

Now that you have the measure of imported words, take heart in the fact that puzzle constructors tend to favor four-letter Anglo-Saxon exclamations. These involuntary ejaculations, uttered by all, are a great fit in the grid:

Puzzle clue: "Butterfingers!"	**OOPS**
Puzzle clue: "That was a close call!"	**PHEW**
Puzzle clue: "I'm in trouble"	**OHOH**
Puzzle clue: "Worrywart's response"	**OHNO**
Puzzle clue: "Attention getter"	**PSST**
Puzzle clue: "Throat-clearing sound"	**AHEM**
Puzzle clue: "Slow down"	**WHOA**
Puzzle clue: "Vocal fanfare"	**TADA**

7

FOUR-LETTER SURNAMES:
Hello, **DALI**

**I feel a special connection to crosswords
because I've become a clue.**

CELESTE HOLM, OSCAR-WINNING ACTRESS AND PUZZLE SOLVER

Which four-letter word answers to all three of the following *puzzle clues:* "Type of oak," "Island located in a river," and "Actress Celeste"? If you guessed **HOLM** (upper- and lowercase **H**), well done. Perhaps best known for her glamorous turn in 1950 as Mrs. Lloyd Richards in "All About —" (**EVE**), she earned her Oscar three years earlier for *Gentleman's Agreement*, the bestseller by Laura Z. Hobson, later puzzle editor at *The Saturday Review.* Co-star of the 1990s soap opera *Loving,* spelling bee champion Celeste **HOLM** became hooked on puzzles during a girlhood of playing Scrabble and looking up words in the dictionary. The Holm family of Long Island was devoted to word games and—with a grandmother in the newspaper business—spelling. For a woman who devoted a lifetime to stage, screen, and UNICEF, crosswords provided a perfect diversion, from what she told me when we chatted about puzzles. Most conducive state in the Union for solving in that performer's professional opinion: California, owing to its laid-back pace. Most fun group to solve with: the crew of any stage production because solving by committee is a bonding experience.

HOLM is proof that in the crossword universe four-letter words reach beyond the lower case. Because Margaret Farrar began to admit celebrity names into the grid, all public personalities with four-letter names have become fair game for the Crossword Hall of Fame. Every puzzle solver comes to recognize repeater names, which means moving further away from the dictionary and getting to know a few dozen monosyllabic surnames. Clue format in this category typically consists of two words: modifier, which describes the occupation, + given name, as in "Actress Celeste." On occasion, celebrity couples who divorce reunite as fellow repeaters. *Puzzle clue:* "Author Roald" (**DAHL**) comes to mind with ex-wife, *puzzle clue:* "Actress Patricia" (**NEAL**). These names also answer, respectively, to more specific puzzle clues that mention their work, such as "*The Witches* author" and "*Hud* Oscar winner." Despite an acrimonious break up, they appear together in the grid without a quarrel.

This category is favored by the Trivial Pursuit whiz who blurts **EDEN** for "TV genie Barbara" or "1950s British Prime Minister" yet pauses to think of the synonym for *paradise*. Puzzle constructors began the name game by drawing from among politicians and world leaders, eventually branching out into the arts. The roster of four-letter names changes with each decade. From Celeste **HOLM**'s generation in a 1966 crossword puzzle edited by Farrar, for example, two four-letter notables appear, an author and a soldier. Herman **WOUK** answers to *puzzle clue:* "Creator of Barney Greenwald," the hero from his Pulitzer Prize–winning book, *The Caine Mutiny* (1951). Attorney Greenwald represents a young naval officer who faces a court martial when he challenges his superior, Captain Queeg. In the 1954 film, José Ferrer plays Greenwald; "Actor Johnson" (**VAN**), the young man; and Humphrey Bogart, evil Captain Queeg.

Another four-letter name of that era is Viscount **GORT** (*puzzle clue:* "British general, hero of Malta"). From County Galway, the sixth viscount **GORT** represented Limerick in Parliament. A war hero, he served in both world wars and ended his career as governor of Malta. The clue refers to his brave defense of the island against the threat of Nazi invasion for which he received the Maltese Sword. In 2007, the ninth viscount **GORT** resides in *puzzle clue:* "Isle of —," you got it, **MAN**, a hot spot on the crossword map. However, the Irish family name has lost steam. Instead, the puzzle solver is more likely to see *puzzle clue:* "Robot from *The Day the Earth Stood Still.*" Nearly eight feet tall, **GORT** was the star of the 1951 sci-fi film and lives on in the Museum of Robots. Of all people, his co-star is a puzzle clue we've already seen: "*Hud* Oscar winner Patricia."

Despite their great accomplishments, since their heyday in the 1960s **WOUK** and **GORT** have faded from the repeater roster because of the unwieldy consonants in their surnames, which do not lend themselves to easy interlock.

■□■□■

Puzzle constructors collect famous names from every industry, era, and country, which sounds daunting until you realize how often these repeaters emerge. Puzzle power hangs on vowels combined with the easy-to-interlock consonants **D, L, M, N, R, S**, and **T**. Crossword creators shout **OLE** (*puzzle clue:* "Corrida cheer") when a surname like **LENO** (*puzzle clue:* "Carson successor") enters the public consciousness. With his puzzle-friendly name, Jay is guaranteed a VIP slot in crosswords, even after he retires from *The Tonight Show*. His appointed successor, **CONAN** O'Brien, is already making himself comfortable in the grid.

The late-night NBC talk show has enjoyed a long-term relationship with crosswords, beginning with *puzzle clue:* "Carson's predecessor" (**PAAR**). The host of *The Tonight Show* from 1957 to 1962, Jack **PAAR** is a welcome double **A** sandwiched between two easy-to-interlock consonants. No matter that he was a loose cannon, sort of an earlier version of *puzzle clue:* "Radio shock jock Don" (**IMUS**). According to TV critic Richard Corliss, talk show history is divided into two eras: Before **PAAR** and Below **PAAR**. For puzzle solvers, the only factor is that he predates Johnny Carson, who hosted the show for twenty-nine years. What about a straightforward puzzle clue like "*Tonight Show* host Jack"? Certainly, it follows the formula of modifier + first name. But without a context, the clue seems ambiguous. The mention of Carson gives a time frame that telegraphs everything the puzzle solver needs to know to ask someone within earshot, "Who was the guy on *The Tonight Show* before Carson?"

Canada's main contribution to crosswords, puzzle repeater Paul **ANKA**, composed "Johnny's Theme," the familiar tune that opens the show. Puzzle clues for **ANKA** span his hits, such as "'Puppy Love' singer" and "'Lonely Boy' singer Paul." His elegant Lebanese surname, a pair of consonants snug between two **A**s, earns him the same longevity in crosswords that he has maintained in the world of pop music.

LENO's late-night competitor, *puzzle clue:* "Letterman," has the advantage of a four-letter first name. He remains the **DAVE** of choice right now, eclipsing the singing partner of the duo "Sam and —." The talk show hostess with the greatest puzzle potential is Emmy Award–winning Kelly **RIPA**. Her co-host on the morning program *Live with Regis and Kelly* calls her by the pet name "Pipa," another candidate for repeaterdom that has yet to filter into crosswords. Slowly, **RIPA** is making her way into the grid. Her show is also a source of future repeaters such as *puzzle clue:* "American Idol winner Aiken" (**CLAY**), who famously clapped his hand over **RIPA**'s mouth on the show.

■ ▪ ▫

To paraphrase the line from the Eagles' hit song "Hotel California," once you check in to the Crossword Hall of Fame you can never leave. Ideally, a repeater surname has both star power and a unique spelling. One example of a repeater blessed with this combination is *puzzle clue:* "People's Sexiest Man of 1999" or " 'Pretty Woman' co-star" (**GERE**). Does anyone not know that Richard **GERE** is a practicing Buddhist and follower of the Dalai Lama, formerly married to supermodel Cindy Crawford? Not even sex symbol Brad Pitt, twice named People's Sexiest Man Alive and owner of two four-letter names, can touch the puzzle power of the consonants **G** and **R** plus **E**. Not only is Brad short on vowels, he's missing the trumping **E**. **GERE** has the staying power that eluded Hollywood puzzle clue: "Producer Mark" (**GERO**), just one vowel from success. *Puzzle clue:* "Liza Minelli's third," **GERO** had his fifteen minutes of crossword fame. It has been reported that Liza enjoyed puzzle solving with her mother, legendary performer Judy Garland, the sort of myth that sticks in the puzzle solver's mind.

GERE is also separated by vowel **O** from politics, *puzzle clue:* "2000 Presidential candidate," "'An Inconvenient Truth' narrator Al," and "2007 Nobel Peace Prize winner" (**GORE**). **GORE** has toppled the *puzzle clue:* "1996 Presidential hopeful Bob" (**DOLE**). Occasionally, Elizabeth **DOLE** made a puzzle cameo when she was head of the Red Cross. In the early 1990s, Bob **DOLE** served as Senate Majority Leader. How neat that his successor in the Senate proved to be another four-letter name with repeater potential, *puzzle clue:* "Mississippi Senator Trent" (**LOTT**). However, with only one vowel, **LOTT** is already past his sell-by date.

Ranking alongside **GERE** is *puzzle clue:* "Hawkeye portrayor" (**ALDA**). Not only has actor Alan **ALDA** received over thirty Emmy nominations but both his first and last names qualify as four-letter repeaters that are compatible in the grid! Since **ALDA** moved on to the big screen, his expanded references include *puzzle clue:* "Star of 'Betsy's Wedding'" and "Oscar nominee for 'The Aviator.'" To confuse puzzle solvers, his father, Tony Award winner for *Guys and Dolls*, sometimes upstages him as *puzzle clue:* "Actor Robert." Robert was born Alfonso Giuseppe Giovanni Roberto D'Abruzzo. The stage name combines the first two letters of his first and last birth names: **AL** + **DA**. What good luck for puzzles that **ALDA** stopped at four letters, rather than going for "Alfdab," which wouldn't be of much use.

No present-day actress matches the puzzle popularity of **ALDA** *père et fils* (French for "father and son"). However, *puzzle clue:* "Silent film star Theda" (**BARA**) ranks for creating another stage name that fans the flame of her memory: **BARA** is short for her mother's maiden name of Baranger. The Sharon Stone of her day, **BARA** was as big in the box office as her contemporary Charlie Chaplin. Of her forty films, with titles like *Sin*, none survives. Yet her name carries on as a four-letter repeater. Her legacy to Crosswordese includes imitators whose names ring a bell for puzzle solvers such as *puzzle clue:* "Silent film star Naldi" (**NITA**), née Anita Dooley of the Ziegfeld Follies, and "Valentino's fiancée Negri" (**POLA**) of Warsaw.

She was born Theodosia Goodman in Cincinnati circa 1885 (she was coy about her birth year), and her stage name, **BARA**, scrambled to create the anagram "Arab death," as her publicists liked to remind fans. Does this imply her lethal impact? **BARA**'s man-hungry style added a modern four-letter word to the English language. With an appetite for men as boundless as a vampire's desire for blood, she was described by the media as a **VAMP**, short for *vampire*, to mean "seductress." This definition of **VAMP** has overtaken the original definition of the word as "The upper part of a shoe." Another **VAMP** who lives on through the power of crosswords is *puzzle clue:* "Mata — (spy)" or "— Hari (spy)." Both names of this alleged World War I spy carry crossword magic. In 1905, Margaretha Zelle of Holland moved to Paris, adopted the stage name **MATA HARI** (Indonesian for "eye of the day" or "sun") and hobnobbed with politicians. Somewhere she went wrong and, during World War I, the French accused her of passing secrets to the Germans. Our leading crossword lady was tried for treason and executed in 1917 at age forty-one. As she faced the firing squad, her final words were said to be, "Merci, monsieur." Rumor has it she wore only a coat to her final public appearance. Was **MATA HARI** a double agent? There is some evidence she was. She was immortalized by Greta Garbo in a biopic, and with two four-letter names, she remains a sweetheart among puzzle creators.

▪▪ ▪ ▪▪

The Spanish surrealist with the famously curlicue mustache, *puzzle clue:* "Artist Salvador" (**DALI**), also answers to "Painter of 'Hallucinogenic Toreador'" and "Painter of 'Persistence of Memory,'" with its melted clocks, a poster perennial in college dorms. How fitting for this playful publicity hound to be immortalized through puzzles. His longtime señora, née

Helena Dmietreevna Deluvina Diakonova, joins him in the Hall of Fame under the succinct four-letter nickname **GALA**. In addition to lower-case **GALA**, *puzzle clue:* "Black-tie event," Señora **DALI** provides a useful alternative. (Her given name wouldn't have gotten her far in the puzzle world.)

The other Spanish surrealist favored by crosswords, *puzzle clue:* "Artist Joan" (**MIRO**), joins the couple as a representative of twentieth-century art. He is associated with *puzzle clue:* "World War I art movement" (**DADA**). Art historians debate whether this four-letter word is the Russian equivalent of Spanish **SISI** (*puzzle clue:* "Agreement in Acapulco") or French slang for "hobby." One thing is certain: **DADA** remains a repeater. **MIRO** also plays a double role in crosswords with two four-letter names. How tricky that his first name, the feminine-looking **JOAN**, is a form of Juan. Very surrealistic!

Spain contributes one more VIP artist to the Hall of Fame, Old Master Francisco **GOYA** of Aragon (*puzzle clue:* "Spanish court painter" or "Maja painter"). Puzzle solvers find his work in the "Madrid museum" (**PRADO**). Despite her crossword-friendly nickname, "Pepa," Señora **GOYA** is absent from the grid. *Puzzle clue:* "Goya subject," however, does appear often: The reference is to **MAIA** (also Maja), a life-size female nude. The model may have been "The Duchess of —" (**ALBA**, now being upstaged by "Actress Jessica"). The risqué paintings were seized during the Spanish Inquisition in the late 1400s and kept under wraps for centuries. No such censorship occurs in crosswords, where **MAIA** and **ALBA** make frequent visits.

■ ▪ □ ▪ ■

The best-known American writer in crossword puzzles is *puzzle clue:* "Author James" or " 'The Morning Watch' author" (**AGEE**). Novelist, screenwriter, and film critic for both *Time* magazine and *The Nation*, **AGEE**'s book *Let Us Now Praise Famous Men* (1941) is widely considered one of the great nonfiction works of the twentieth century. His book documents eight weeks the author spent among sharecroppers in Alabama with photographer Walker Evans in 1936. The wordy title is unfortunately too long for a standard clue, which explains why his short autobiographical novel, *The Morning Watch*, has become the reference point. The Tennessee-born writer was also a screenwriter on the classic 1951 Humphrey Bogart film *The African Queen*. **AGEE** received the Pulitzer Prize posthumously for his novel *A Death in the Family*. Although he died young in 1955, while en route to a doctor's appointment in a taxi, his name lives on for puzzle solvers.

The American playwright worth knowing for crossword purposes is *puzzle clue:* "Playwright William" or " 'Picnic' playwright" (**INGE**). Known as the "playwright of the Midwest," **INGE** milked his hometown of Independence, Kansas, for material. He won the Pulitzer for *Picnic*, which became a classic film in 1955 with William Holden and *puzzle clue:* "Actress Novak" (**KIM**). The prolific playwright penned a series of 1950s classics familiar to puzzle solvers: *Come Back, Little Sheba*; *Bus Stop*; and *Splendor in the Grass*. *Puzzle clue:* "Actress Natalie" (**WOOD**) co-starred in the latter with Warren Beatty, a newcomer whose six-letter surname puzzle constructors have little use for.

The first half of the twentieth century produced two female authors of note for puzzle solvers, beginning with "Writer Anita" or "'Gentlemen Prefer Blondes' author" (**LOOS**). Thanks to her 1925 bestseller, Anita **LOOS** has maintained her rank in the Crossword Hall of Fame. A suffragette, this writer was a staunch supporter of the Lucy Stone League. Lucy Stone believed that women ought not to take their husbands' name after marriage, further insurance that **LOOS**'s name would carry on in puzzles. It is interesting to note, in light of this fact, that her 1928 sequel, *But Gentlemen Marry Brunettes*, sank like a rock. **LOOS**'s fellow female writer answers to *puzzle clue:* "Author of 'The Fountainhead'" (**RAND**). **RAND** created objectivism, a lifestyle philosophy that continues to draw followers. Her unique first name, **AYN**, doubly ensures her high profile in puzzles. Her bestseller is the missing-link *puzzle clue:* "— Shrugged" (**ATLAS**). Née Alisa Rosenbaum, **RAND** is another puzzle repeater who chose a crossword-compatible pseudonym.

As for nonfiction, the winner is *puzzle clue:* "Author Shere" (**HITE**) of the *Hite Report*, the 1970s study of female sexuality. Apologies to Dr. Ruth, another expert on the subject, whose four-letter professional name does not have the grid appeal of the well-endowed double-voweled **HITE**.

■ ▬ ■

Four-letter baseball stars in the Crossword Hall of Fame hail largely from the Dominican Republic, beginning with **A** for **ALOU** (*puzzle clue:* "Baseball family name" for the outfield trio Felipe, Jesus, and Matty). A second Dominican surname that shot to prominence since 2005 is **SOSA**. What a pleasure to have an alternative to the stale old standard removed by one vowel, **SOSO** (*puzzle clue:* "Middling"). While with the Texas Rangers, Sammy **SOSA** made baseball history in June 2007 by hitting his six hundredth home run. He is only the fifth player ever to achieve that record and the only one born outside of the United States. Until this pair of four-letter surnames made sports history, the answer to *puzzle clue:* "Baseball name of fame" was predictably three letters: **OTT**, for right fielder Mel of the Giants. Ambidextrous **OTT** batted with his left hand and pitched with his right. He remains unchallenged in the three-letter category.

Sportswomen of crosswords include *puzzle clue:* "Agassi partner" or "Five-time US Open champ" for Steffi **GRAF**. The puzzle solver welcomes the tennis couple of the Louis Vuitton print ad campaign rather than facing the traditional clue: "— Spee," for **GRAF** Spee, the World War II battleship named after a German admiral. The other female *puzzle clue:* "Soccer star Mia" gives us the double **M** for **HAMM**. Thanks, Mia, for keeping women's soccer alive and kicking through puzzles, and for giving puzzle constructors an understudy for "Actress Farrow."

In our celebrity-driven era, when reality television challenges the average viewer's ability to keep up with names, puzzle constructors have a bigger pool than ever from which to choose potential repeaters. Celebrities from the 1990s like rap star "Snoop —" (**DOGG**) and "Actor Jared" (**LETO**) of TV's *My So-Called Life* are still a flash in the puzzle pan. **AUEL** (*puzzle clue:* "Jean creator of 'Clan of the Cave Bear'") is gaining momentum but is not yet more than a blip. *Puzzle clue:* "Newscaster Paula" was working wonders for **ZAHN** while she was on CNN, but can she sustain the momentum post CNN? It could be argued that getting an on-air position is easier than entering the Crossword Hall of Fame with a four-letter **Z** name.

It is impossible to predict the shelf life of a puzzle name. For example, surnames with serious puzzle power like Theda

BARA outlive the reputation of their owners. In my early days of solving, I greeted *puzzle clue:* "Author Willard" (**ESPY**) like an old friend. In the 1980s he was known as the author of *Word Puzzles: Anagrams from America's Favorite Logophile.* (Anagrams are jumbles, or letters scrambled to make two different words, as **GORE** to **OGRE**.) **ESPY** produced more than ten books of light verse that incorporated wordplay. With some prescience, he published this letter to the editor in his book "Another Almanac" (1981):

> Sir or Madam:
>
> For an autobiography, I should be grateful for recollections from anyone who can remember me.

His claimed intention was to send this to the *New York Times Book Review*. With few twenty-first-century puzzle solvers aware of his doggerel, **ESPY** has been replaced by the dictionary *puzzle clue:* "Catch sight of" or, more succinctly, "Spot." In the final analysis, *Webster's* is a formidable opponent in the world of clues.

8

FOUR-LETTER FIRST NAMES:
Who's Who in Clues

Finding my name in the crossword would be so gratifying,
I'd have to retire.

ROY BLOUNT JR., *WAIT, WAIT…DON'T TELL ME!* PANELIST
AND PUZZLE SOLVER

Membership in the Who's Who of Clues is guaranteed by a unique, world-famous first name with puzzle-friendly letters such as *puzzle clue:* "Humor writer Blount Jr." (**ROY**). Good-bye *puzzle clue:* "Cowboy Rogers" of old-time television! In conversation with "Author Blount Jr." about his addiction to puzzles, he blamed "The Gold Bug," Edgar Allan Poe's cryptogram-laden story, for giving him a taste for solving in boyhood. Predictably, he graduated to the cryptic crossword with its riddle-type clues. His impressive jumble-solving skills, he told me, referring to the newspaper pencil game, enable him to unscramble the letters to make sense in a flash. That's the ultimate payoff for years of anagram solving.

Another prime example of a winning four-letter first name is **DEMI**, short for Demetria, *puzzle clue:* "Actress Moore." Once upon a time, her name answered to the dull dictionary term: "Half: pref." Replace the **M** for **S** to answer *puzzle clue:* "First name in '50s comedy," or **DESI** Arnaz, husband of comedienne Lucille Ball. And no matter how many times Charlie Chaplin wed, *puzzle clue:* "Mrs. Chaplin" is always **OONA**, the Gaelic form of her mother's name, Agnes. Daughter of playwright Eugene O'Neill, **OONA** Chaplin was the actor's final spouse and mother to his eight children. The quirkiest four-letter name answers to *puzzle clue:* "Woody's son" or "A Guthrie" (**ARLO**). The western Massachusetts–based folksinger **ARLO** built a career on his eighteen-minute, twenty-second 1967 song "Alice's Restaurant Massacre." Arlo's female counterpart is early Hollywood star **ZASU** Pitts, born in Kansas more than one hundred years ago. Her parents combined the last letters of Eliza with the start of Susan to satisfy family members, and unwittingly made a major contribution to Crosswordese. It is unlikely that any of this quintet will be toppled, thanks to their one-of-a-kind four-letter names. Same for single-named pop stars **CHER**, **DIDO**, and **ENYA**. Well chosen!

Foreign names afford a measure of clue longevity, as with these *puzzle clues:* "Sitarist Shankar" (**RAVI**), "Composer Bartok" (**BELA**), and "Tennis's Nastase" (**ILIE**). Nastase's name also serves as the last two words of the rhetorical question, *puzzle clue:* "Would —?" The Vatican provides two candidates: **PIUS** and **LEOI** (*puzzle clue:* "The Sainted Pope"). How clever of puzzle constructors to include Roman numeral **I** to create a four-letter word from a three-letter name, ending in a vowel. Using the same principle, puzzle solvers now connect **ACTI** to *puzzle clue:* "Play opener."

Two middle names play a major role in crosswords, each starting with **A**. One graces the rock-and-roll legend, Elvis, whose middle name is **ARON**. How fortunate that a man with so much charisma contributes a variant spelling for puzzle constructors. He is one letter removed from "Scientologist Hubbard" (**LRON**), another boon for puzzle constructors. The other middle name of repeaterdom is *puzzle clue:* "**TAE** part" (**ALVA**), as in Thomas **ALVA** Edison. A lightbulb moment!

Crosswordese favors four-letter first names ending with **A**, as illustrated by these repeaters:

Puzzle clue: "Author Ferber" or "Poet St. Vincent Millay"   **EDNA**

Puzzle clue: "Author Bombeck"   **ERMA**

Puzzle clue: "Swenson of Benson"   **INGA**

Puzzle clue: "Author Jaffe" or "Columnist Barrett"   **RONA**

No longer just a name for authoresses, **EDNA** has two fresh puzzle clues, thanks to cross-dressing: "John Travolta role" (Mrs. **EDNA** Turnblad in *Hairspray*), and "Dame — Everage," Barry Humphries's alter ego known for outrageous eye wear.

In the early days of crosswords on March 15, 1914, *World* newspaperman Arthur Wynne ran *puzzle clue:* "Short for Dorothy" (**DORA**). The name has all the hallmarks of an excellent four-letter word, but it needed a viable puzzle reference. Not until 1999 did the Public Broadcasting Station come to the rescue with its hit kiddie show about a Mexican girl. In the interim decades, **DORA** was *puzzle clue:* "Picasso's muse" (née Henriette Theodora Markovitch), whose portrait sold for $95 million in 2006. What about Freud's patient named **DORA**? The teenager struggling with depression and other issues is bad news and, therefore, is kept at arm's length. These days, every puzzle solver gets **DORA** for the missing-link *puzzle clue:* "— the Explorer."

For **ROB**, Wynne offered boring *puzzle clue:* "An abbreviation of a boy's name." Almost a hundred years later, puzzle solvers expect to see *puzzle clue:* "Actor Lowe" or "Lowe of 'The West Wing.'" There was a time when the puzzle clue referred to the screen husband of Mary Tyler Moore on *The Dick van Dyke Show*. More fun as a nickname than in its verb form, *puzzle clue:* "Stick up."

Census polls and crossword constructors universally agree on the most popular girl's name: **EMMA**. Cluewise, she gives the puzzle constructor choices. From fiction there are multiple *puzzle clues:* "Jane Austen character" and "Gwyneth Paltrow role" as well as "Madame Bovary" or "Flaubert heroine." From pop music there is *puzzle clue:* "Baby Spice" aka **EMMA** Bunton. (Baby Spice, incidentally, is the mum of baby **BEAU**, who may one day make his own mark in crosswords.) Off-screen, **EMMA** is Oscar-winning *puzzle clue:* "Actress Thompson" of the Harry Potter series and *Love Actually*. In her college days, Thompson was romantically linked with *puzzle clue:* "Actor Laurie" (**HUGH**) of the Fox series *House*. But his name is not even in the top one hundred repeaters.

Scroll from **EMMA** to number twenty-four for a familiar name to puzzle solvers: **ELLA**. Puzzle constructors thrive on repeater **E** names ending in **A** separated by a double consonant. For puzzle solvers, **ELLA** is predictably *puzzle clue:* "Singer Fitzgerald" or "Scat singer." (*Scat* describes a jazz style of improvised singing, in which the singer replaces words with syllables to imitate a musical instrument.) Fitzgerald recorded with superstars Count Basie and *puzzle clue:* "Ellington" (**DUKE**). Winner of armloads of Grammies, *puzzle clue:*

"The First Lady of Song" dominated among four-letter first names without challenge. In summer 2007, hit song "Umbrella" by Rihanna introduced a possible challenger. It includes a chorus of lower-case **ELLA**s. Longest-reigning single in a decade, the rainy-day song made music history and spawned a line of umbrellas. The other four-letter jazz singer who hugs a double consonant between **E** and **A** is **ETTA** (*puzzle clue:* "Singer James"), best known for her hit "At Last." She cannot touch **ELLA**, however, for appearances in the crossword.

At number twenty-five we find a three-letter repeater: **AVA**. This name belongs to 1950s screen siren, *puzzle clue:* "Actress Gardner." The daughter of a North Carolina tobacco farmer, she ended up in Hollywood, famously married to Mickey Rooney, jazzman Artie Shaw, and Frank Sinatra, in that order. "Old Blue —" (**EYES**) recorded the song "I'm a — to Want You" (**FOOL**) after their breakup. **AVA** marches onward in crosswords, sometimes described as star of *The Barefoot Contessa* (1954) or *Night of the Iguana* (1964). The name is back in circulation. The star of *Legally Blonde—puzzle clue:* "Actress Witherspoon" (**REESE**)—has named her daughter **AVA**, so with any luck she may one day step in as the clue.

Scroll on. Pass number twenty-nine, **LILY**—*puzzle clue:* "A Munster" (the sitcom of yore) or "Actress Langtree" (mistress to Edward VI)—to number thirty, **ANNA**. The palindromic name answers to *puzzle clues:* "Sigmund Freud's daughter" and

Tolstoy's classic "— Karenina." A host of actresses answer to **ANNA**, from Italy's Magnani to young Oscar-winner Paquin. In the 1930s, Anjuschka Stenski Sudakewitsch of Kiev Anglicized her name in an attempt to compete with Garbo. By the time producer Samuel Goldwyn cast her in the film based on *puzzle clue:* "Zola bestseller" (**NANA**), she called herself **ANNA STEN**, two four-letter words that have entered the lexicon of Crosswordese. *Times* crossword editor Will Weng was fond of *puzzle clue:* "Author Emile" (**ZOLA**). He and his scandalous book about a courtesan, **NANA**, were standard repeaters. Perhaps due to the current interest in J. M. Barrie, as portrayed by *puzzle clue:* "Actor Johnny" (**DEPP**) in *Finding Neverland*, this four-letter repeater has a new spin. It now is seen as *puzzle clue:* "Peter Pan dog."

Leapfrog over Allison to number thirty-eight: **MAYA**. In crosswords, there is just one *puzzle clue:* "Poet Angelou," author of *I Know Why the Caged Bird Sings*. She is a few slots ahead of the three-letter **MIA** (*puzzle clue:* "Mamma —"), which, of course, is also recognizable as *puzzle clue:* "Actress Farrow."

■ ▬ ▬ ■

For decades, the puzzle-friendly **EDIE** had one standard *puzzle clue:* "Comedienne Adams," from the early days of television. Together with her husband, **ERNIE** Kovacs, **EDIE** entertained

America in the late 1950s. He smoked Muriel cigars, which she promoted in commercials with the suggestive line: "Why don't you pick one up and smoke it some time?" (Old **ERNIE** has been upstaged by the orange-faced *puzzle clue:* "Sesame Street resident" or "Bert's friend," rumored to be romantically linked.) The fragrant **EDIE**, meanwhile, has been erased by five high-profile namesakes:

> *Puzzle clue:* "Actress Falco." Known by television viewers everywhere as Tony's wife, Carmela, on *The Sopranos*, she attended college with actor **VING** Rhames, who may yet break into crosswords with his unique four-letter given name.

> *Puzzle clue:* "Sedgwick of the '60s." The Warhol "Factory Girl" has been re-created as *puzzle clue:* "Sienna Miller role" from the 2006 film. This **EDIE** is distantly related to *puzzle clue:* "Actress Sedgwick" (**KYRA**), from the TV series *Closer*. However, a four-letter word starting with **K** cannot catch up to one beginning with **E**.

> *Puzzle clue:* "Pop singer Brickell." Current wife of musician Paul Simon, this **EDIE** is the lead singer of the New Bohemians. She met her husband on *Saturday Night Live* (**SNL**).

> *Puzzle clue:* "Role in the musical 'Grey Gardens.'" The 2006 show *Grey Gardens*, based on the 1975 Maysles

documentary about the cousins of Jackie Onassis, recounts the story of Big **EDIE** Beale and her daughter, Little **EDIE**. The first documentary ever to become a Broadway show, it revived the missing-link clue for the four-letter color **GREY**.

Puzzle clue: "Nicollette Sheridan role." The award-winning series *Desperate Housewives* provides a roster of four-letter names, starting with **EDIE** Britt, the serial divorcee played by Sheridan. Marcia Cross plays **BREE** Hodge, with the double **E** of a good puzzle co-star. **TERI** (*puzzle clue:* "Actress Hatcher") trumps "Actress Garr" of *Tootsie* fame. **EVA** (*puzzle clue:* "Actress Longoria") has erased all memory of her predecessor, "Actress Gabor," co-star of the classic sitcom *Green Acres*.

As for boys' names, the U.S. Census shows that parents are no help to Crosswordese: The top three names—Jacob, Aidan, and Ethan—each count five letters. Still, we find *puzzle clues:* "Actor Quinn" (**AIDAN**), from *Legends of the Fall*, and "Actor Hawkes" (**ETHAN**), the ex-husband of "Actress Thurman" (**UMA**). Neither is more than a blip on the scope. Number four, at last, **RYAN**, counts four letters. The father of the actress Tatum (*puzzle clue:* "Actor O'Neal") has been a perennial puzzle star. Of course, **RYAN** is also seen as *puzzle* *clue:* "Actress Meg," which gives the name even more puzzle promise.

At number five, Matthew yields **MATT**, with its useful double **T** and a pair of *puzzle clues:* "Actor Damon" and "Actor Dillon." Thanks to *The Bourne Legacy* and *People* magazine, Damon is in the lead. The small screen supplies *puzzle clue:* "Longtime name on 'Today.'" Tricky since Katie comes to mind before co-host **MATT** Lauer. (Apologies to both.) *Puzzle clue:* "Drudge of the Internet" for the website that dishes the dirt in politics is yet another option for **MATT**. From TV reruns there is *puzzle clue:* "Detective Houston" played by actor Lee Horseley. This mustachioed **MATT** (short for Matlock), first to carry the clue, was a millionaire private eye who was surrounded by a bevy of bathing beauties while solving crimes. His uncle was played by *puzzle clue:* "Actor Buddy" (**EBSEN**) aka "Barnaby Jones actor" and, way back when, "One of the Beverly Hillbillies."

Leap to number twenty-one, **NOAH** (*puzzle clue:* "First name in dictionaries"). He plods on as *puzzle clue:* "Biblical figure" or "Ark builder." Hollywood has a new contender with "Director Baumbach" (**NOAH**), whose award-winning screenplay for *The Squid and the Whale* made waves. Number thirty-two, **EVAN**, answers *puzzle clue:* "Author Hunter," although "Politico Bayh" with its unlikely **YH** ending is a contender. Separated by one consonant is *puzzle clue:* "Actor McGregor" (**EWAN**). With his memorable double-voweled name, the English actor has the look of a puzzle star. Finally, at number forty is the four-letter **SEAN**, which for decades belonged to *puzzle clue:* "Actor Connery." Younger Seans have muscled in with *puzzle clues:* "Actor Penn" and "P. Diddy."

Where puzzle constructors are concerned, the top boy's name is undoubtedly **ALEC** (*puzzle clue:* "Actor Baldwin"). Co-star of *30 Rock*, **ALEC**, eldest of four thespian brothers, lords over Daniel, William, and Stephen, all counting too many letters. The U.S. Census ranks the similar name **ALEX** at number forty-seven, as in *puzzle clue:* "Baseball's Rodriguez." But **ALEC** is the name of crossword choice. Baldwin has a couple of decoys—namely *puzzle clues:* "Guinness" and an obscure British actor, "Actor McCowen." Baldwin's ex-wife, *puzzle clue:* "Actress Basinger" (**KIM**), is seldom seen.

Puzzle constructors also favor **OMAR**. In the era before Will Weng, he mainly appeared as *puzzle clue:* "A tentmaker." World War II, a seemingly bottomless pit of four-letter words, offers *puzzle clue:* "General Bradley." Born in a Missouri log cabin, **OMAR** Nelson Bradley graduated from West Point at the top of his class and ended his career as the last surviving five-star officer in the United States. He commanded three corps on D-Day. After *Dr. Zhivago* came out in 1965, however, *puzzle clue:* "Actor Sharif." Three cheers, therefore, to newcomer, *puzzle clue:* "Actor Epps," who plays Dr. Eric Foreman on the Fox series *House* and gave twenty-first-century puzzle solvers a new **OMAR**.

9

THREE-LETTER WORDS:
The Shortest Repeaters

**I could have been a poet if I'd worked
on meter instead of 1 Across.**

E. J. KAHN JR., *NEW YORKER* STAFF WRITER AND PUZZLE SOLVER

Of the many high-profile puzzle solvers I've met over the years, journalist E. J. Kahn Jr. was the most competitive. He was forever discussing record times and working on his own game. His approach was that of a golfer, applied to the pencil game. He vividly recalled the woman who enticed him to take up puzzles in his youth: the wife of the director of the Theater Guild, Mrs. Munsell. He even tried his hand at construction, which he found onerous and no fun at all compared to puzzle solving, four-letters inclusive.

At this juncture in our survey of Crosswordese, the

discerning reader must question if there is more to crossword puzzles than four-letter words. Predictably, the answer is yes: Expert puzzle solvers have mastered a parallel lexicon of three-letter words, which is perfect symmetry for a game tailor-made for the three-letter **FUN** section of the *New York World*. Arthur Wynne, the word game genius who dreamed up this twentieth-century obsession in 1913, preprinted the letters **F, U,** and **N** into three boxes at the top of his debut grid to illustrate the fill-in process. When he put his first crosswords together, one- and two-letter words were acceptable in pyramid-shaped grids. By the time the crossword turned fifty, three letters became the minimum in the 15 × 15 grid layout.

If pressed to select a three-letter term that dominates the category, puzzle constructors would find it a toss-up between the noun **ADO** and the verb **EKE**. That useful **D** connecting two vowels answers to a variety of straightforward *puzzle clues:* "Bustle," "Brouhaha," and "Hubbub" as well as the missing link in Shakespeare's comedy, "Much — About Nothing." It is always helpful for puzzle constructors to have a choice when dealing with a garden-variety repeater like **ADO**. Change the initial vowel to create the two-word repeater **IDO**, which mainly answers to *puzzle clue:* "Wedding vow." One more initial vowel switcheroo yields *puzzle clue:* "Tokyo, once" (**EDO**). Familiar to fans of *Shogun,* **EDO** is the old name for Tokyo.

Although the **EDO** period of Japan ended in 1868, it lives eternally in the repertoire of puzzle solvers.

Three-letter verb **EKE** has been around since the time Athelstan ruled England in the 900s. It answers to *puzzle clue:* "Scrape by, with 'out'" because it requires the auxiliary adverb. When you're "on your uppers," as the Victorians used to say about folks who were too poor to replace the soles of their boots, you eke out, but when you scrape, you scrape by. Its homonym, the Anglo-Saxon exclamation **EEK**, generally connects to a puzzle clue like "Reaction to a mouse" or "Fearful sound." It derives from the world of the funny papers and television cartoons, which produced a purple cat in the 1990s called **EEK**. Or open **KE** with another vowel to find the missing link to a campaign slogan from the 1950s in *puzzle clue:* "I like —" (**IKE**). President Eisenhower has given way to a modern-day **IKE** (*puzzle clue:* "Turner of music"). Together with ex-wife, the four-letter **TINA**, they made rock history in 1966 with their hit "River Deep—Mountain —" (**HIGH**), which *puzzle clue:* "Producer Spector" (**PHIL**) considered his best work. The three remained in the headlines for reasons outside their musical talents. One more initial vowel change transports the puzzle solver to Hawaii, which, as we've learned, is the most repeater-rich state of the Union. *Puzzle clue:* "Luau instrument" leads to **UKE**, short for *ukulele* (Hawaiian for "jumping flea"). This "Guitar's cousin" sparked national attention in 1915 when it crossed over to the mainland, thanks to Tin Pan Alley and vaudeville performers. *Puzzle clues:* "'Tiptoe through the Tulips' singer" and "Tiny —" (**TIM**) based his musical success in the 1970s on his trusty **UKE**.

A three-letter repeater that is fizzling after an extended run is **NEE** (pronounced *nay*). Past particle of the French verb meaning "born," it is used to introduce the maiden name of a woman, as in *puzzle clue:* "Hillary Clinton, — Rodham." Originally, it answered *puzzle clue:* "Wedding announcement word" from the days when a bride routinely assumed her husband's surname. Although its double **E** works well in the woof and weave of crosswords, as a concept it has lost support and now answers to the literal *puzzle clue:* "At birth."

Some repeaters start to fade but can make a comeback with a new definition. Such is the case with the oddball **RET**. For decades, it trudged along as the archaic verb of *puzzle clue:* "To soak, as flax." As Mrs. Shakespeare of Stratford-upon-Avon knew, flax makers submerged hemp in water to separate the fibers. One vowel away from **ROT**, the **RET** process entails partial rotting before the fibers become pliable. Linen making has been superseded by a military *puzzle clue:* "Abbr. after a general's name." With the same three letters, but meaning "retired," the puzzle editor puts a new spin on the old standby, turning the verb into an adjective with more relevance to the puzzle solver's world.

While four-letter words dominate among the thirty answers of the premier 1913 puzzle, crossword inventor Wynne threw in a couple of baby words, *puzzle clues:* "A boy" (**LAD**) and "The plural of is" (**ARE**). Dullsville! To balance them, he challenges the audience with the obtuse *puzzle clue:* "The fibre of the gomuti palm." (His British upbringing is one explanation for the transposition of the final letters in *fiber.*) Gomuti is just the sort of absurd-looking tongue twister that irritates the easily discouraged solver. More recognizable by its four-letter synonym **SAGO** (*puzzle clue:* "Variety of palm tree" or "Palm type"), the trunk of the gomuti supplies the fibers, or **DOH**, which are used for thatching roofs in tropical climates.

With no experience in thatched roofs, the modern puzzle solver is justified in finding this word exasperating. Same word, different era: After fading out of sight for eighty-five years, **DOH** has been redefined by the cartoon character Homer Simpson, who has turned the word into an attractive three-letter crossword repeater. Accompanied by a tap to the forehead, **DOH** is Homer's characteristic reaction, meaning "Obvious! Why didn't I realize this?" For crossword purposes, the answer drops the apostrophe because punctuation marks have no place in the grid. Current *puzzle clue:* "Homer's head-slapping remark." Any school child with a passing knowledge of *The Simpsons* will readily call out the answer. They also realize that Homer is not a reference to the ancient bard.

In 2001, sixty-seven years after adding the term "crossword puzzle," *The Oxford English Dictionary* officially invited **DOH** into the language, defined as an "expression of frustration." It even includes an alternate spelling, which has begun to infiltrate crosswords, **DUH**. Puzzle constructors owe a big thank-you to actor Dan Castellaneta, who provides Homer Simpson with his voice, for the distinctive delivery of the annoyed grunt that created a fresh puzzle clue from an archaic term that debuted in the very first crossword.

Six weeks into the new game, Wynne published an editorial note by the February 1 crossword puzzle in the Fun section, soliciting contributions:

> Fun's crossword puzzles apparently are getting more popular than ever. The puzzle editor has received from readers many interesting new cross-word puzzles, which he will be glad to use from time to time. It is more difficult to make up a cross-word puzzle than it is to solve one. If you doubt this, try to make one yourself.

With this short note Wynne introduced the concept of freelance contributions that instantly became the industry standard. The response to this mild dare was overwhelming and ensured the longevity of the game. Millions of people who solve puzzles every day rely on a few hundred professionals to provide this number one pastime. Computers have helped expedite production in recent years, but brain power and a sense of humor are still essential.

When scanning clues from 1914, that first year of crosswords, what stands out is how often puzzle constructors enlist the three-letter repeaters that continue as the currency of the modern crossword. Between the first crossword and today's version, the balance of world power has shifted, nations have divided and reconfigured, terrorism has taken on new dimensions, **ETC** (*puzzle clue:* "Common list ender, for short"). Yet the three-letter words that appeared in the first crossword nearly a hundred years ago carry on, untouched.

In fact, the language of Crosswordese predates the square grid. The equilateral shape became the norm when the crossword celebrated its tenth birthday in 1923. Early puzzle constructors were flamboyant in their designs, forming grids into a variety of frameworks, like arrows and diamonds. Modern crosswords require overall interlock of letters from top to bottom, so that each letter operates in two words. By contrast, many early efforts consist of mini grids of three or four words across connected by bands of black squares like islands in a dark sea. Often a single letter appears alone, like an **ISLE**.

In 1923, when Margaret Farrar became serious about her responsibilities for the crossword corner at the *New York World*, she developed and instituted industry standards. Newspaper readers recognize the visual presentation: iconic square, an odd number of boxes across and down, symmetrical black-and-white pattern and columns of clues. Farrar set the cap on number of black squares in the diagram to one-sixth maximum (thirty-eight in a 15 × 15 grid). In the second *Cross Word Puzzle Book* of 1924, the editors note, "A too black pattern means the constructor was a bit lazy." It is easier to glue tiny groups of four-letter words with rows of black boxes than to weave together strands of twelve-letter words. Friday and Saturday crosswords in the *New York Times* often feature extended parallel rows of blank boxes, sometimes fifteen letters across. This is the signature of the virtuoso puzzle constructor.

■ ▬ ▬

Vowels, it's clear, are the reason words become repeaters in both the three- and four-letter categories. In order to interlock gracefully, the puzzle constructor needs a generous dollop of **A**'s and **E**'s to alternate with commonly used consonants. Before the crossword celebrated its first birthday on Christmas Day 1914,

R was the obvious connector of **A** and **E** (*puzzle clue:* "The plural of is"). The drawback with **ARE** is that there is no opportunity for cleverness. It works best as a missing-link clue. For ages, it was a reference to the 1972 Goldie Hawn romantic comedy, *puzzle clue:* "Butterflies — Free," inspired by a line in Charles Dickens's *Bleak House.* In recent times, the three-letter verb is more often set in a quotation, as from Thomas Paine *puzzle clue:* "These — the times that…" The phrase ends, "try men's souls," which puzzles often do. Despite its congenial letters, puzzle solvers don't encounter **ARE** as often as its four-letter repeater relations, the perennial river **AARE** and *puzzle clue:* "Type of code" (**AREA**). More often **RE** is introduced by **I** (*puzzle clue:* "Wrath").

Puzzle solvers of the *World* crossword would be tickled to see the trio of durable three-letter repeaters: **ACE**, **ALE**, and **ATE**. In 1914, **ACE** answered to *puzzle clue:* "Title given a distinguished aviator." Same old repeaters, different decade! **ACE** continues in its pilot context, although references extend to tennis seeds such as Swiss player "Roger Federer, for one." The final noun option is the playing card, as in *puzzle clue:* "King topper." Of course, **ACE** can be an adjective in answer to *puzzle clue:* "Top-notch." Finally, as a verb, students understand that if you **ACE** a course, you are in the top percentile. As for **ALE**, Wynne offered the literal definition, *puzzle clue:* "A liquor made of malt." **ALE** for puzzle solvers now answers to the perennial "Pub order," which is sometimes the clue for the four-letter word **PINT**. For variety, the repeater masquerades as "Toby filler," in which *toby* is a drinking mug with a jolly man's face from King George's day. Originally, Wynne presented **ATE** simply as *puzzle clue:* "Did eat." Slang gives the option of dressing up this otherwise dull repeater with *puzzle clue:* "Chowed down." Lightly disguised, it also appears in a colloquial term as "Cooked at home, with 'in.'"

Crosswordese is heavy on **A** + consonant + **E** repeaters. Leading the way is one that is rarely spoken—*puzzle clue:* "Summer cooler" (**ADE**). Sometimes presented as "Suffix with lemon or lime," the word ending has eclipsed the fact that it was once a famous surname. Gone are the days of *puzzle clue:* "Humor writer George," bestselling author of *Fables in Slang.* A wag from Wynne's day, **ADE** was known for quips such as, "Anybody can win unless there happens to be a second entry."

Equally ubiquitous is *puzzle clue:* "Imitate" or "Copy" for **APE**, as a verb. Add an **R** to make it a four-letter word, *puzzle clue:* "Copycat" for **APER**. Rounding out the group is *puzzle clue:* "Latin greeting," **AVE**, meaning farewell. More often this three-letter term doubles as an English abbreviation, *puzzle clue:* "St. crosser" or "5th, e.g." The shortened form for *street* implies that the answer is curtailed, short for *avenue.*

Puzzle people read the news with an eye for different items. When Shinzo **ABE** was elected prime minister of Japan in

2006, for example, puzzle constructors filed the name as a useful alternative to *puzzle clue:* "Pres. Lincoln" or "Fortas of the Supreme Court," who served in the late 1960s. Perhaps not the most honest **ABE**, the Senate accused Justice Fortas of improprieties. When President Lyndon Johnson nominated him to succeed Earl Warren as Chief Justice, the Senate put him on the hot seat in a manner that changed the way public figures were held accountable. Ultimately, Warren E. Burger got the job, thanks to President Nixon, but **ABE** Fortas is still the man in puzzles. Meanwhile, Prime Minister **ABE** (two syllables: *ah-bay*) faced an equally rough time during his one-year tenure in 2007. Four members of his cabinet resigned and another committed suicide. Yet, he has a chance at crossword immortality. But, then, **B** in the second position is not particularly desirable for a three-letter repeater, with the exception of **OBI** (*puzzle clue:* "Kimono sash" or the more evocative "Geisha's sash"). A key component of traditional Japanese attire, this strip of fabric holds the kimono closed.

U.S. presidents are a natural subject for crosswords, as witnessed by *puzzle clue:* "George W., for one." The reference is to **ELI**, a colloquial term for a Yale student. Remarkably, since 1972 each presidential election has included a candidate with a Yale diploma, from Gerald Ford to Hillary Clinton. The three-letter perennial **ELI** made its debut well before the Bush tenure, appearing in the June 14, 1914, crossword. The original puzzle clue was "A proper name used for a college." The name dates to an early endowment by merchant Elihu Yale. (A man named Dummer was even more generous to the school; but, as the story goes, when considering a name change, the Collegiate School of Connecticut opted for Yale.) Yale made his fortune with the British East India Company, apparently not all of it legitimately. What better way to exonerate himself than by bankrolling an institution of higher learning? His good intentions, and his crossword-compatible nickname, have been rewarded amply. *Puzzle clue:* "Actor Wallach," **ELI** of puzzles past, is taking a backseat to the Ivy League.

＊　＊　＊

During World War I, banal *puzzle clue:* "Space of time" yielded the three-letter repeater, **ERA**. Sixty years along, the Equal Rights Amendment legislation, intended to ensure equality for both sexes under the Constitution, came close to ratification. The intention was to strengthen the Nineteenth Amendment, which grants women the right to vote. Perhaps it did not find support in Congress, but among puzzle constructors the **ERA** remains meaningful. Since 1979, puzzle solvers have come to see *puzzle clue:* "Failed amendment letters." Perhaps it's not funny or witty, but it is a good alternative to *Webster's* clue of "Historical time." This differentiates it from the other three-letter time span, **EON**, and its variant spelling, the four-letter **AEON**, which is closer to its Greek roots. An **EON** (*puzzle clue:* "Long historical time") comprises two or more geological **ERA**s.

Another vowel + **RA** repeater that's familiar among baby boomers is **IRA**. In Wynne's time, **IRA** answered to *puzzle clue:* "A boy's name." Since 1974 the letters have acquired a new definition thanks to the Employee Retirement Income Security Act (ERISA). Puzzle solvers understand the reference to individual retirement account, a modern version of a pension. "Retirement fund initials" has become a standard clue, trumping *puzzle clue:* "A Gershwin," brother of the composer George and lyricist for "The Man I Love," "Embraceable You," and "I Got Rhythm." Those songbook standards need no further promo from crosswords. However, on a Friday you may see *puzzle clue:* "Actress von Furstenberg." This **IRA** (née Virginia Carolina Theresa Pancrazia Galdina), former sister-in-law of designer Diane von Furstenberg, is alternatively described as a socialite.

———

Two repeaters that resonate for sports fans as well as puzzle fanatics are common cries of support. In English-speaking countries, *puzzle clue:* "Arena cheer" means **RAH**. This second syllable of *hurrah*, when doubled, becomes the adjective *rah-rah*, an Americanism that describes the spirit captured by leaping cheerleaders.

Same sentiment, different sport, as we saw in the chapter about armchair travels, *puzzle clue:* "Corrida cheer" (**OLE**). Alliteration is favored in the clue structure, to repeat a stylistic preference mentioned earlier in the book. Derived from Arabic, the Spanish word of encouragement is comparable to the English four-letter word **EGAD**, in that it invokes Allah in an acceptable manner. Facing the toreador is the four-legged, four-letter repeater, **TORO**. As I've already told you, the bull may bow to the lawn mower manufacturer by the same name, which introduces a new dimension to the puzzle clues. Adhering to Farrar's rule of good news preferred in puzzles, the image of newly cut grass definitely appeals more than the notion of a bull in the ring.

━━━

Puzzle constructors borrow three-letter combinations from the most mundane sources. A card in your wallet, for example, carries your **SSN** (Social Security number), *puzzle clue:* "Some personal data: Abbr." Double **S** in the first position makes this an ideal repeater along the bottom row at the end of three words. Indeed, the letters work just as well for puzzle constructors as for the **IRS**. This institution works together with *puzzle clue:* "April VIP" (**CPA**).

The shoe store seems an unlikely provider of puzzle material, yet delivers a well-worn repeater, **EEE** (*puzzle clue:* "Wide foot" or "Shoe spec"). Triple **A**, on the other hand, answers to *puzzle clue:* "Battery," or the financial "Top bond rating." The way the wind blows supplies a variety of combinations like **ENE** and **SSW**. Rather than the vague *puzzle clue:* "Vane direction," the modern puzzle constructor cites an example with coordinates as in "Dallas-to-Austin dir." (You can decode the abbreviation by now.) Incidentally, when the Concorde pulled the **SST** out of the sky in 2003, this action affected more than jet-setters: It meant the shutdown of a high-flying repeater.

The telephone keypad is a source of three sequential letters. Because most people carry cell phones, it's easy to verify the answer to *puzzle clue:* "Phone trigram." The number 6 yields puzzle-friendly **MNO**. It's a nice respite from typical *puzzle clue:* "Letters after L" or "L followers." Call letters from radio and television continue to feed the three-letter category. Listeners of *Weekend Edition*, the radio show that features puzzle master Will Shortz, tune in to **NPR** (National Public Radio) every Sunday at 8:40 a.m. for a dose of puzzle wit. These are the folks who easily answer *puzzle clue:* "Home of 'The Diane Rehm Show'" or "'A Prairie Home Companion' airer." Similarly, TV viewers have the advantage when faced with "Home of 'The Sopranos'" or "'Curb Your Enthusiasm' airer." Is there a Rip van Winkle among us who does not know the answer is **HBO**? Two consonants plus a vowel ending guarantees more viewers in crosswords than a string of consonants like **NBC**.

Broadway provides three letters that are music to a theater producer's ears: **SRO**. *Puzzle clue:* "Sellout letters" represents the cheap seats, as in standing room only. Because *angel* is slang for investor, the trickier clue for this answer is "Good sign for an angel." (**SRO** also means "single room occupancy," or flophouse, less often cited in clues.) Angel leads to **STE** (*puzzle clue:* "Holy woman: Abbr.") She may be referenced as in "Jeanne d'Arc, e.g." Or the same three letters answer to a missing-link *puzzle clue:* "Sault — Marie," the oldest city in Michigan, founded in 1668. Twinned with the city of the same name over the border in Ontario, together the cities are called the Soo. The phrase translates as "The rapids of St. Marys," the river that connects Lake Superior to Lake Huron. Despite the S-double-**O** combination, it is not a hit in crosswords.

The most recognizable three-letter sequence worldwide is the distress signal, **SOS**. In Wynne's day, it answered to *puzzle clue:* "A wireless call." Yes, the wireless and the crossword are contemporaries. Morse code came up with the concept of **SOS**, which became official in 1908. Everyone knows that the initials represent the message "Save our souls," meaning "Survivors on shore." In truth, the phrase was developed as a memory device after the sequence was devised.

Pop music gives us a better way to define **SOS** than "Help!" Pop singer Rihanna to the rescue yet again! Her 2006 number one hit works, all about her plea for assistance. This is the same

Rihanna who, as we know, won crossword attention with the refrain **ELLA** the following year. Her choice of lyrics is music to a puzzle constructor's ears. Fresh clue material for age-old repeaters keeps the game youthful.

10

BRITISH FOUR-LETTER WORDS:
Cryptic Crosswords

These puzzles are on a wavelength only dogs can hear.

RICHARD MALTBY JR., BROADWAY DIRECTOR
AND CRYPTIC CONSTRUCTOR FOR *HARPER'S*

I only know of one song titled "Crossword Puzzle," which belongs to the Broadway show *Starting Here, Starting Now*, lyrics by Richard Maltby Jr. In it he tells the story of a woman who lost her boyfriend due to her superior puzzle-solving powers. Tragedy! (Has the puzzle-minded reader noted the spate of juniors among the puzzling elite of the last three chapters, namely Blount Jr., Kahn Jr., and Maltby Jr.?) Maltby once told me that he approaches musicals as very large puzzles, since a lyricist has to be as structured as a constructor. In his case, he is referring to the British cryptic crossword with its double entendres, anagrams, and other forms of wordplay, with

which he has been entertaining the readers of *Harper's* magazine for decades. As a boy who spent his free time copying
words out of the dictionary, he figures ending up on the constructor's side of the puzzle was a logical progression.

Puzzle clue: "Playwright George Bernard" (**SHAW**) famously
observed how England and the United States are two countries "divided by a common language." The remark applies
even to the crossword clue. When the word game crossed the
Atlantic in the 1920s, Shaw would have been pushing seventy
and primed for another quarter century of quips. The crossword he would have solved was unlike Arthur Wynne's. Yes, it
involved a grid plus numbered clues, but it lacked the complete
interlock and neat columns of clues. Instead, the playwright
would have worked a 15 × 15 grid with up to fifty-seven black
squares—twenty more than permitted to American puzzle
constructors—and with wordy clues! The extra black squares
fence in some letters so that they are "unchecked," or belong to
only one word. Or Shaw might have faced a 12 × 12 grid of all
blank squares, known as a "barred grid," punctuated by bold
lines to indicate where words end. In both cases, the clues look
like sentences, *look* being the operative word. By contrast to
the straightforward synonym clues connected with four-letter
words, British clues set out to stump the puzzle solver.

Wynne's crossword landed in the pages of England's *Pearson's Magazine* in February 1922. This forward-thinking

publication had first released H. G. Wells's *War of the Worlds* twenty-five years earlier. The word game instantly captured the imagination of E. Powys Mathers, a contemporary of *puzzle clue:* "Pound of poetry" (**EZRA**) and a translator of classic Sanskrit texts. His translation of *The Book of a Thousand Nights and One Night* has remained in print for seventy years. Fluency in Sanskrit came in handy for a man who was about to ramp up the conventional crossword.

In place of dictionary definitions, Mathers devised a clue system that synthesized puns and anagrams—in other words, double entendres and scrambled words. After testing it among a select group of friends, he polished one for the *Saturday Westminster*, which published it in 1925. The following year, London weekly newspaper the *Observer* hired him. As a promotional gimmick, the editor offered readers the chance to win a prize for sending in the correctly completed crossword. Clipped-out grids arrived by the cartload, confirming that Mathers had struck a chord with the audience. Until his death in 1939, the poet and translator pursued a parallel career, setting nearly seven hundred cryptics for the *Observer*. At the same time, the *Observer* also provided the "Everyman Puzzle," a version of the general-knowledge American-style crossword.

To go with the cryptic flavor of his work, Mathers adopted an alter ego: Torquemada, the Spanish Grand Inquisitor. This dramatic nom de plume set the precedent for his successors at the *Observer*: Ximenes and Azed. (Current puzzle constructors call themselves Quixote, Mephisto, and Fidelio.) Pressed by his audience to create new challenges, Torquemada came up with the bar diagram, rejecting symmetry and complete interlock. With his wife's assistance, Mathers estimated that a typical cryptic took two hours to produce from start to finish. His wife described him as a "relaxed Buddha" who worked in bed. Mrs. Mathers was rightfully proud of the fact that no matter how often the same word appeared in a Torquemada cryptic, it always was accompanied by a fresh clue—four-letter words included.

Wordplay drives every clue, which explains why the British crossword is called *cryptic*, as in "mysterious, terse, and encoded." Clue structure dominates the British version, whereas American crosswords prefer to doodle with graphics, like drawing a heart into a single box to take the place of the five-letter **HEART**. Rather than matching synonyms, the cryptic crossword introduces one more dimension: Each clue works as a mini puzzle, offering both a synonym and a devious clue. The only given is the number of letters in the answer, which appears in parentheses at the end of the clue. Even the term for puzzle constructor changes: The British refer to *puzzle setters* or *compilers*.

How deviously Torquemada and company camouflage their answers! But there is a method to the madness: The handful of clue styles conform to written rules, using "signal" words that direct the puzzle solver. Take the book title *puzzle clue:* "Pretty girl in crimson rose (8)," by cryptic puzzle solver Sandy Balfour. This clue converted him from an amateur to a fan. The only known from the clue is that the answer is eight letters long. Code words indicate the deciphering process. In this case, the code word is *in*: It signals that one word will be inserted into another to spell the solution. Scan the clue in this manner: "Pretty girl / in / crimson / rose." Rather than a noun, *rose* is a verb and the definition of the answer. *Pretty girl* or **BELLE** placed "in" *crimson* (**RED**) yields a synonym of *rose*: **REBELLED**. Nothing in the result has to do with a young lady in a pink outfit. An American puzzle constructor would use *puzzle clue:* "Rose." After tackling this clue, the puzzle solver fully appreciates how British cryptologists were equipped to crack the Wehrmacht Enigma code during World War II!

The cryptic loses the American puzzle audience right at this point. Who can be bothered with this type of clue? Puzzle solvers who know their four-letter words and are ready for the next level. The upside of a code is the fact that a code exists. With practice, it is possible to decipher British puzzle clues. The process is a bit like traveling to England: Americans get the chance to hear their language spoken with a different inflection. The approach is adapted from Lewis Carroll via an exchange between Alice and the March Hare: "You need not mean what you say, but you must say what you mean." No matter how absurd the clue appears at first glance, once the puzzle solver cracks the shorthand of the code, everything makes sense.

There are fifteen types of cryptic clues, each containing a synonym and a riddle portion. When you read the clue, you must first suspend judgment. The second step is to determine which sort of clue it is by looking for signal words. Typically, the first or last word in the clue is the straightforward synonym. Here is a sampling of the clue types to give you the flavor of how they work:

- Anagrams (scrambled words)—*puzzle clue:* "Scot fractured a leg (4)." The signal word *fractured* indicates scrambled letters. The four letters for the answer are supplied in the clue: *a leg*. A synonym for *Scot* that uses the letters **A, L, E,** and **G** is **GAEL**. Signal words for anagrams include *broken, confused, mixed up,* and *twisted.* The American style clue would stop at "Scot."

- Hidden words (consecutive letters within the puzzle clue)—*puzzle clue:* "In Jodphur, a lazy river (4)." Ignore the comma. Pay attention to the signal word "in." Examine the letters from adjoining words to connect *Jodphur* to *a lazy*, and find the four-letter **URAL**. Nothing to do with the Indian city but rather one of crossword's top four-letter rivers that flows from Russia into the Caspian Sea. Signal words are *in* and *inside*.

- Container clues (two words, one inserted into another)—*puzzle clue:* "Horse galloped around ring (4)." *Ring* is code for the letter **O**, a ring shape. Place it inside a synonym for *galloped*, or **RAN**, to yield the *horse* **ROAN**. Signal words include *around, holding, inside,* and *within.* For an American-style crossword clue, the word "Horse" would do.

- Double definitions (two synonyms)—*puzzle clue:* "Talk about African land (5)." Split the clue in half for two ways of defining the same answer. A five-letter *African land* (country) is **GABON**, which is also the two words **GAB** and **ON** for *talk about.* As with American crosswords, two-word phrases dispense with the break. No signal word is the giveaway.

- Reversals (the answer word is spelled backward)—*puzzle clue:* "Return of tendency to correct (4)." A four-letter word meaning *tendency* is a synonym for *to correct* when spelled from left to right. Reverse **TIDE** to get the four-letter repeater **EDIT**. Signal words include *backward, return,* and *the wrong way.*

- Homophone (two words sound alike but are spelled differently)—*puzzle clue:* "Spooky-sounding lake (4)." No doubt the most popular lake in all of crosswords is the one with the eerie sounding name, **ERIE**. Signal words are *aloud, oral, sounds like,* and *they say.*

- Charade (connect syllables to form a larger word)—*puzzle clue:* "Bird that is a character on 'Sesame Street' (5)." The first syllable of the answer is a *bird,* the sea eagle or **ERN**; the second is *that is* or **IE** for the Latin *id est.* Together they add up to an orange guy or *character on Sesame Street* named **ERNIE**. Since a charade is a word chain, sometimes there is no signal word, which is a signal. Possible signal words are *leads, after,* or *follows.*

- Deletions (a word loses a letter to yield the answer)—*puzzle clue:* "Beheaded celebrity is sailor (3)." A repeater, the three-letter **TAR**, meaning *sailor,* results when **STAR** (*celebrity*) is *beheaded,* a signal word for losing the initial letter. For an end letter, the signal word is *tail.*

Where is the lexicon of four-letter words? Sorry, folks, they play no comparable role in the British version of the game. Neither is there a theme that links three or four puzzle answers of more than ten letters each. Although the **OED** (*Oxford English Dictionary*) contains all the answers that appear in the typical British crossword, it offers little support to the puzzle solver. You cannot look up *puzzle clue:* "Pretty girl in crimson rose (8)."

For the all-American puzzle solver, the reason to understand the British mind-set is its code. Thanks to Will Shortz and his supporters, indicators from the cryptic clue system have been borrowed by American clues. These words replace the traditional tags *prefix* and *suffix* and liven up some of the most mundane four-letter words. Here is a roundup of the main suspects:

> *Introduction* replaces *prefix,*
>   as in "Introduction to a cure?"   **PEDI**

> *Beginning* replaces *prefix,*
>   as in "Cultural beginning?"   **AGRI**

> *Closing* replaces *suffix,* as in "Poll closing?"   **STER**

> *Finale* replaces *suffix,* as in "Major finale?"   **ETTE**

A question mark at the end of a clue acts as a tip-off to a dash of wit. The puzzle solver grasps that the suffix **STER** answers to *puzzle clue:* "Poll closing?" It's more satisfying than the *puzzle clue:* "Suffix with poll." For the ambitious puzzle solver, *The Atlantic* features a puzzle by the prolific crossword team of Emily Cox and Henry Rathvon; Richard Maltby Jr.

(*puzzle clue:* "'Ain't Misbehavin'' director") compiles cryptics for *Harper's* magazine. Even for the *puzzle clue:* "— in the wool" (**DYED**) American puzzle solver who intends to shun the British crossword (which would be a shame), an understanding of how like-minded people across the Pond solve puzzles can sharpen your pencil.

One by one, Fleet Street newspapers added a crossword feature—most notable, in 1930, was the *Times of London*. (In 2004, the *Times* unleashed another newspaper puzzle feature upon unsuspecting solvers: the number-placement puzzle that Shortz describes as a "crossword without words," which was a staple in American magazines for decades under the name Number Place. Repackaged as the Japanese phenomenon called Sudoku, it is now available in books and most newspapers.) There were few puzzle constructors to call on at that time. In desperation, the *Times of London* approached the puzzle constructor of the general-knowledge *Observer* crossword, Robert Bell. Bell felt his son Adrian could handle the job. Author of a bestselling book (*Corduroy*) about his farm near Bury St-Edmunds, young Bell rose to the challenge. Against a ten-day deadline, he came up with an acceptable submission. From that day for almost half a century, Adrian Bell constructed cryptics for the *Times of London*, in total creating about five thousand puzzles. His identity was a well-guarded secret for forty years, upon which anniversary the newspaper unmasked their popular puzzle constructor. He confirmed, as per Mathers at the *Observer*, that a wife's help is "essential to a setter" (puzzle constructor). In the final analysis, Bell told the interviewer that "you must be near dotty to spend your life setting crosswords." His daughter, Anthea Bell, has chosen as her life's work a comparable literary career as the translator of the acclaimed *Asterix* comic series.

The British public is spoiled for choice with newspapers, each of which has a distinct political slant. But whether Labour or Tory, every newspaper includes at least one cryptic. According to level of difficulty, beginning with the easiest and ramping upward, the sequence escalates from right wing to left: the *Daily Telegraph*, most popular; the *Times of London*, best known and most strictly edited (also sponsor of an annual contest); the *Independent*, regarded as "innovative"; and the *Guardian*, among whose setters it counts Crispa, who contributed from 1954 until her retirement in 2004. On Sundays, the *Observer* carries on the tradition, catering to both ends of the spectrum with the Everyman and a cryptic by Azed. On Sunday, the *Times of London*, the *Telegraph*, and the *Independent* feature two cryptics apiece.

The cryptic code is so specific, there is no debate once the puzzle solver gets the answer word. Take a Cox and Rathvon double definition clue for **FARE**: "Progress with diet (4)." Grasping that the answer functions as both a verb and a noun, the answer is clear. In a conventional puzzle, *puzzle clue:* "Diet" could elicit a different four-letter **F**-word—namely **FOOD**. Due to that ambiguity, American puzzle solvers rely on intersecting answers to confirm their answers. The cryptic lexicon also includes a lengthy list of signal words that follow the code, such as *ring* to mean **O**.

Once the puzzle solver becomes familiar with the shorthand, parsing the clues is as easy as pie—or could it be pi?

11

Four-Letter Words
Outside the Box:
Crossword Variations

Did you ever notice how the name Alec Guinness
can be jumbled to read "Genuine Class"?

DICK CAVETT, TALK SHOW HOST AND PUZZLE SOLVER

Dick Cavett is one of those guys who can take the letters of your name and come up with a quip using the same letters. In his own case, he rearranged his name, Richard A. Cavett, to read Catch It a Rare VD. His knack is so involuntary, he told me, that sometimes he wakes up and realizes he is making them up in his dreams. He discovered this talent when he was introduced to a board game called Perquacky, a sort of spill-and-spell game. He is not alone in this affliction. At the Stamford Crossword Tournament one year, the way E. J. Kahn recorded it, one of the contestants came up to me and said,

"Am Hitler clone." He was not, however, speaking of himself but the letters of my name. I suppose he suffers from the same anagramitis as Cavett.

Crosswords are square, but their variations are not. The zigzag diagramless puzzle made an unexpected debut in 1925 at a Manhattan trattoria, while the rectangular acrostic was born a decade later after a Wellesley College reunion. Like Athena from the head of Zeus, the latter concept leapt fully formed from the imagination of an occasional constructor, who hurried home to Brooklyn to capture a literary crossword puzzle on paper. It is not surprising that Wellesley alumnae permeate celebrity three- and four-letter repeaters, with *puzzle-clues:* "Author Ephron" (**NORA**) in the lead, trailed by "Actress MacGraw" (**ALI**), and the newsworthy "Senator Clinton, — Rodham" (**NEE**). A Wellesley candidate for repeaters in the five-letter category is Mary Martha Corinne Morrison Claiborne Boggs Roberts, or *puzzle clue:* "NPR journalist Roberts," aka **COKIE**. A grid-friendly choice of nicknames wins puzzle points again.

While father of *puzzle clue:* "Singer Simon" (**CARLY**), Richard Simon, and his partner, Max Schuster, rushed the first crossword bestseller back to press, Farrar and company stumbled upon a diabolical concept: It was the act of puzzle solving **SANS** (*puzzle clue:* "Without") the familiar black-and-white grid. Turning back the clock to 1925, as recalled by

Farrar (then Petherbridge), she was checking a manuscript after lunch with collaborator F. Gregory Hartswick when they encountered an unattached clue list. With the responsibility for a puzzle empire, Farrar was committed to quality control and personally proofread every grid for errors. **ALAS** (*puzzle clue:* "Expression of woe"), how to solve without a diagram? The editors were sipping espresso at Moneta's Italian restaurant in lower Manhattan, and no one offered to run back to the office in those pre-BlackBerry days. Instead of panicking, Hartswick, aka "Gregorian," embraced the production error. Four years earlier, *puzzle clue:* "Playwright Pirandello" (**LUIGI**) penned *Six Characters in Search of an Author*, and now Hartswick had clues in search of a diagram. Sketching a grid on the back of the menu, he worked out the pattern by filling in the answers and shading in the black squares—and the rest is crossword history. Water glasses clinked as the editors dubbed this new version of crosswords the "diagramless" and introduced a new dimension to that innovative **ERA** (*puzzle clue:* "Important time") of puzzle madness.

It is curious that the *New York Times* diagramless puzzle has appeared below the Sunday crossword for decades, yet its followers represent a mere fraction of the puzzle audience. The extra effort of determining placement of numbers and black squares requires a commitment beyond the scope of the average Sunday puzzle solver. In the opinion of 1960s television panelist Henry Morgan, from *puzzle clue:* "What's My —?" (**LINE**), diagramless puzzles are most suited for the housebound. The exception to this theory is newspaperman Ben Bradlee, who knocked off numerous diagramless puzzles at his desk during lunch when he was editor of the *Washington Post*. He confessed to me not only that diagramless puzzles were his favorite but also that he threw out the grid to transform a conventional crossword into a diagramless. What he realized early on was this tidbit of insider scoop: The diagramless relies heavily on repeaters. **YEAH** (*puzzle clue:* "Slangy assent"), basic Crosswordese makes diagramless puzzles tick. Because the point of the exercise is to uncover the grid pattern, puzzle constructors ease up on the answers and even bulk up on black squares. To further compensate for the absent diagram, the puzzle editor waters down the clues. Do I hear **RAH** (*puzzle clue:* "Football cheer")?

Neurobiologists believe that this system of solving backward, from clues to diagram, stimulates right-brain thinking. Whereas the left brain focuses on verbal information (names, facts, and figures), the nonverbal part of the brain is stimulated by visual puzzles of this type. Creating the pattern balances the mental workout. Approach the diagramless as a jigsaw puzzle that uses letter sequences in place of cardboard pieces: As an **ISLE** (*puzzle clue:* "Capri, for one") of interlocked words emerges, the puzzle solver slots it together with the adjacent piece, like chunks of a jigsaw, to complete the picture. Four-letter words stored in the left brain come to the fore as the right brain sketches out the diagram.

To solve a diagramless, your first step is to scan the clue list for old familiars and jot them in the margins right next to the clue. Finally, a showcase to flaunt your command of four-letter words! Follow the same sequence as with solving a conventional crossword. Once you've drained the clue list, check the top of the page for the puzzle dimensions, phrased as a multiplication equation. The standard measure for the *New York Times* is 17 × 17, counting seventeen boxes Across and Down (which earns the puzzle constructor $225, 20 percent more than the daily 15 × 15). The grid outline tells the puzzle solver nothing about the pattern within, so keep an eraser handy.

As Farrar always advised, for best results start at 1 Across with a diagramless. Two indicators reveal the number of letters in this answer: The number of the next Across clue and the numbering of the first Down clues. For example, if 5 Across follows 1 Across, the answer for 1 Across consists of four letters. Solve for 1, 2, 3, and 4 Down to develop the first chunk of the puzzle. When working a sequence of Down words, letters in the horizontal rows begin to spell out Across answers. The puzzle solver may then assign numbers to answers that appear Across only. The big unknown is in which column of the top row 1 Across starts. To borrow the old real estate slogan: Location, location, location! Nothing in the puzzle itself indicates placement of 1 Across. For this reason, some publications (including the *New York Times*) offer a hint to position this first word. Hints never appear on the page with the puzzle (that would be too much of a giveaway), but are printed elsewhere, for those who want a jump-start. Otherwise, make an arbitrary decision and select a spot on the top row of a sheet of graph paper.

Like the conventional crossword, the pattern for the diagramless tends to follow rotational symmetry so that the pattern in the top left corner mirrors the bottom right corner, and the top right corner mirrors the bottom left. But beware: Diagramless constructors have the alternative option of left–right symmetry. Furthermore, the cap on black squares rises to allow puzzle constructors whimsical diagram patterns that resemble familiar objects, like a pinwheel or a lantern, bulging out in the middle with only one word at the top and bottom. Sometimes the grid is X-shaped, with two words at opposite corners divided by a string of black squares. A quick way to gauge how much open space the diagramless contains is to count number of clues. The typical 17 × 17 may contain from seventy-four to ninety words, with the lower figure indicating bigger islands of black squares.

Determining where numbers and black squares belong in

the diagramless requires a methodical system. Here are five basics of grid construction that make solving simpler:

- A number appears in the first square of each answer, both Across and Down.

- A black square appears before the first letter of an Across answer (unless it abuts the border of the grid).

- A black square appears at the end of an Across answer · (unless it hits the right-hand border).

- A black square appears at the end of a Down answer (except along the bottom row).

- Across and Down clues share a number when they share a first letter.

On Sundays, the *Times* generously supplies a blank grid with its diagramless in an effort to tempt puzzle solvers who do not have graph paper on hand. Beginner diagramless puzzle solvers are best off using the hint for 1 Across, such as: "The first word starts three boxes in." This means filling in three squares along the top row. If 1 Across reads *puzzle clue:* "Sitarist Shankar," the solver then places **RAVI** in boxes four through seven, with numbers 1 through 4 above and to the left of each letter. Thanks to the Beatles and *puzzle clue:* "Singer Jones"

(**NORAH**), who happens to be Shankar's daughter, many puzzle solvers have heard of the Indian musician. The answer also fills in the first letters for 1 through 4 Down; so, after a bit of doodling, the puzzle solver can then begin to see where the pattern leads.

—■—■—

When the crossword turned five, the Great Depression hit the United States. Oddly enough, the economic downturn delivered a boost for a game that provided hours of entertainment for the cost of a newspaper and a pencil. A pair of like-minded New Yorkers took advantage of this **ERA** (*puzzle clue:* "Important time") to lead the crossword in new directions. Architect Alfred M. Butts designed a board game he called Criss Cross (short for *criss crosswords*), which caught on when renamed Scrabble after World War II. His experimentation started with the Victorian parlor game of anagrams and a box of alphabet tiles. The object of that game is for players to create words by combining selected tiles. Butts adapted this concept with a 15 × 15 cardboard grid to marry the elements of chance with crosswords. To determine how many tiles of each letter were needed, he studied letter frequency on the front page of the *New York Times*. Based on the measure of Scrabble set sales, his formula of one hundred tiles—ninety-eight letters (including a dozen **E**'s) plus two blanks—was a stroke of genius.

As Butts fiddled with lettered tiles in Poughkeepsie, New York, a teacher named Elizabeth Seelman Kingsley was similarly occupied in Brooklyn. Spurred to action after her Wellesley reunion, she despaired that students embraced twentieth-century scribblers like James Joyce. Tailoring a crossword grid, she stretched its boundaries to create a rectangle. Taking an excerpt from a favorite author, she filled in the grid reading left to right only; words were separated by black squares and continued below and to the left when necessary. Each blank square was assigned a number from 1, at the top left, to 178, at the bottom right corner. Her first selection was six lines from the poem "Ulysses" by Alfred, Lord Tennyson, to upstage the dreaded Joyce:

> And tho
> We are not now that strength which in old days
> Moved earth and heaven, that which we are, we are.
> One equal temper of heroic hearts,
> Made weak by time and fate, but strong in will
> To strive, to seek, to find and not to yield.

Spelling out the poem in anagram tiles, she threw all 178 letters into a pot. From this alphabet soup she pulled out eighteen letters for the poet's name and seven for his work, which she set down in a column. In the style of an acrostic puzzle, these four words provided the first letters for a system of twenty-five anagrams. She adapted this concept from poems by the idols of her youth, Edgar Allan Poe and Lewis Carroll, who composed valentines with the first letters of each line connecting to spell the name of a beloved.

Rather than clue every single word, she took the inspired step of combining letters to create longer answers. She divided clues into two columns. The definitions, or synonyms, were followed by a series of numbers to indicate where the answer letters belong in the grid. The words column consisted of blank spaces in which to jot the answer. (In the modern version of the puzzle, the definition is followed by a series of dashes above numbers that indicate grid placement.) Definitions for this type of puzzle are solved outside the grid in an extra step unrelated to the excerpt: The puzzle solver writes the answers in the blank spaces and then transfers each letter of the answers to its assigned place in the grid.

As the grid begins to fill up, the puzzle solver may guess at missing letters in the excerpt based on English syntax: three letters with central **H** becomes **THE**; three letters with a final **U** is always **YOU**; three letters beginning with **A** can be **ARE** or **AND**, depending on what precedes. Single letters are a choice between **I** or **A** and are seldom an initial. Russell Baker feels that the pleasure of solving the crostic is in recognizing the speech patterns as they emerge. Working backward, the puzzle solver can transfer the letters **T**, **H**, and **E** from the grid to their places next to the definitions. Once the puzzle solver has most of **ALFRED**, answering the rest of the author's name becomes possible. When the puzzle is complete, the solver discovers the quotation, author, and source for a satisfying puzzle experience.

Despite her efforts to marginalize Crosswordese in her work, Kingsley could not keep the double crostic completely free of four-letter words! Her very first published double crostic starts with five-letter repeater **ATTAR** (*puzzle clue:* "A perfume of roses"). Experienced puzzle solvers recognize this Persian term for what is commonly called rose oil. In the Crostics Club column that she wrote to accompany her puzzle, Kingsley acknowledged how repeaters help crossword puzzle constructors out of a bind, especially when the letter **H** is concerned. English sentences contain them in massive numbers. She wrote her fans: "Do you realize that H's are the bane of my existence, being as common as they are, and that H's predominate in Greek, Hebrew, Hindu and other Oriental words?... If you were constructing a puzzle and had letters left over and they made a Vedic deity, what would you do?" When it comes to four-letter words, puzzle solvers are forgiving.

Six months of nonstop production yielded a manuscript of a hundred double crostic puzzles. In March 1934, Kingsley left the pages at the offices of *The Saturday Review of Literature* (a spin-off from the book supplement of the *New York Post*) with an editor by the friendly name of Amy Loveman. On a Tuesday, the contract was signed; and soon after, Kingsley set up shop at the Henry Hudson Hotel, where she personally crafted a weekly puzzle from her home office. Simon & Schuster gave her a series, and she introduced an acrostic feature for the Sunday *Times* puzzle page. The D-C (as it was originally known) holds special appeal for humorists: Ogden Nash credited it with saving his sanity while on the lecture circuit, and Russell Baker claims it helped him kick a tobacco habit. Norman Cousins, editor-in-chief of *The Saturday Review* from 1942 to 1972, believed the D-C "is to crosswords as chess is to checkers." Cousins was in a position to judge: He supervised the evolution of the D-C for the duration of his tenure.

Unlike the crossword, which draws from freelance puzzle constructors, one constructor produced every single double crostic. Kingsley was succeeded in 1952 by her assistant, Doris Nash Wortman, a former president of the National Puzzlers' League, who died suddenly after fifteen years on the job; she was followed by actor Thomas H. Middleton. Although Cousins was related to Middleton by marriage, the selection was made independently by author Laura Z. Hobson (*Gentleman's*

Agreement) in an anonymous solving contest. From 1967, Middleton continued his puzzle career even after *The Saturday Review* folded in 1986, producing acrostics for the Sunday *Times* puzzle page until 1999 and continuing the Simon & Schuster series. Middleton produced the original puzzle samples in Taipei, while on the set of *The Sand Pebbles*, with *puzzle clue:* "Film director Robert" (**WISE**). As with four-letter words, there is an economy of characters in the crossword universe.

12

FOUR-LETTER WORD DASH:
Solving Against the Clock

You go to a movie set and you might have a gut-wrenching scene or you might be sitting all day doing the crossword puzzle.

MATT DAMON, MOVIE STAR AND PUZZLE SOLVER

Finally, crosswords have a sex symbol! Action man Jason Bourne, aka *puzzle clue:* "Actor Damon" of Harvard, is a speed-demon solver. He revealed his puzzle abilities in a press release interview prior to the release of *The Bourne Identity* in June 2002. A man who can wield an **EPEE** (*puzzle clue:* "Three-sided blade") when portraying a Brother Grimm ought to be able to **DICE** four-letter words! **KUDOS** (*puzzle clue:* "Accolades"), Matt, for joining the **FRAT** (*puzzle clue:* "Rushing group") of celebrity solvers. (Is one **KUDO** feasible, in light of the fact that *kydos* is technically singular, Greek for "praise"?)

I believe the hobby shed its **ANILE** (*puzzle clue:* "Old womanish") reputation when cool Jon Stewart of *The Daily Show* revealed his crossword obsession in the Patrick Creadon documentary *Wordplay* (2006). Judging by the tournament players who were interviewed in the film, the demographics definitely skew toward the **MASC**. What a relief that Creadon has hard evidence that crossword devotees extend beyond everyone's mother and me.

What we stand to learn from Damon's remark about keeping a crossword going while on set is his puzzle-solving technique: He solves in stages. Nibbling at a crossword remains one of life's simple pleasures, even for the BlackBerry generation. Puzzle solving feeds on interruptions, even responds well to a short absence. Sometimes the gray matter needs a break to allow the memory bank to make a successful withdrawal. Take the four-letter baseball surname **AL – –** that eludes you in the morning. After lunch, you recall the final vowels to complete **ALOU**, outfielders Felipe, Matty, and Jesus. Felipe's son with repeater potential, **MOISES**, carries on the family tradition because he belongs to four-letter *puzzle clue:* "N.Y. team" (**METS**). Erstwhile Mets first baseman Keith Hernandez sharpened his solving skills in the 1980s at four-letter **SHEA** (*puzzle clue:* "Queens Stadium"). The way he explained it to me, Hernandez paced himself with the goal of completing three-quarters of a puzzle in one sitting before the game and polishing it off after. By the end of his tenure with the Mets, Hernandez upped his puzzle intake to two a day: the *Times* in the a.m. and the *New York Post* in the evening.

Self-restraint can be as challenging for puzzle solvers as it is for dieters. "Bet you can't eat just one" applies to the puzzle appetite as aptly as to those who can't resist **LAYS** (*puzzle clue:* "Popular potato chip"). Once in *puzzle clue:* "Land of temptation" (**EDEN**), some people become "Totally smitten" (**GAGA**) with crosswords. Musical geniuses seem particularly susceptible to the charms of crosswords. Seven-time Tony-winner Stephen Sondheim introduced cryptic crosswords to Leonard Bernstein when they collaborated on *West Side Story* in the mid-1950s, and later to the wider American audience via *New York* magazine. He claimed in a 2004 London interview to have gone cold turkey on crosswords due to the "addictive" quality of the puzzle passion. Diva Beverly Sills confided in me that she savored crosswords in the wee hours, as a sort of puzzle nightcap. She tucked a stash of them in her wallet to counter insomnia while traveling. Imagine her pleasure every time she came across four-letter word **ARIA** (*puzzle clue:* "'Eri tu,' e.g.") before lights out.

■ ▪ ■

As puzzle solvers gain experience, they raise the bar. For the commuter, the challenge is to complete the crossword within a measured span of time. Suburban trains are rife with pen-sporting puzzle solvers setting personal records. Award-winning staff writer for *The New Yorker* E. J. Kahn Jr. allocated the last ten minutes of his journey south into Grand Central Station to a personal race through the *Times* crossword. His technique was to keep the crossword under wraps until the train pulled into 125th Street. Upon the announcement that doors were closing, he flipped to the daily crossword; and, as the train pulled into its next and last stop, he was crossing the last **T**. His sociable nature yearned to introduce another dimension to the game. In a solving race with Bel Kaufman (author of *Up the Down Staircase*), according to the version he told me, he completed the entire Sunday *Times* puzzle page from top to bottom well ahead of her. He considered chal-lenging fellow solver Russell Baker to a puzzle race when both were named Literary Lions at the New York Public Library in the same year. Whether it came off is doubtful.

Stamford, a few stops along the Metro north from Kahn's home, was the site of the annual crossword weekend from 1978 to 2007. Creadon follows the 2005 tournament in *Word-play*, capturing the camaraderie among the few hundred contestants. That year was also made memorable by the dark-horse winner: Rensselaer Polytechnic student Tyler Hinman, youngest ever in Stamford Tournament history. Hinman's introduction to crosswords dates to a fateful Friday in ninth grade. Although that *Times* crossword was too difficult for him to complete, he was whizzing through the clues by Monday—or so he thought. He got a comeuppance later, when he realized it wasn't that he had improved but that the puzzles are easier before Thursday.

For four consecutive years, Hinman has claimed first place, earning $5,000 in 2008 (up from $1,000 in prior years) for a weekend of puzzle solving under pressure. He is the only puzzle speed solver to **ACE** four in a row. New Yorkers David Rosen (1983, 1985–1987) and Jon Delfin (1989–1991, 1995, 1999, 2002–2003) have passed the top slot back and forth, along with Chevy Chase, Maryland, resident Douglas Hoylman (1988, 1994, 1996, 1997, 2000). After graduation, Hinman became a bond trader in Chicago. Women don't seem to fare as well in competitive solving, by the measure of Stamford's results. Only in the launch year, 1978, did women take both first and second places, receiving prizes from Mrs. Farrar herself. Nancy Schuster from Rego Park, New York, went from first grand-prize winner to become editor-in-chief of Official Publications, the puzzle magazine conglomerate, as well as a judge at subsequent Stamfords. Second-place-winner Eleanor Cassidy of Fairfield, Connecticut, seems to have retired from competitive solving after taking the silver.

The public puzzle weekend is a race through seven 15 × 15 puzzles in total. I last participated in the Eighth Annual Stamford Crossword Invitational (1985) and ranked 58th out of 126 contestants. That year the winner, David Rosen, grabbed the $400 purse. (In recent years, armchair athletes have begun to solve at their own pace from home, online.) The Stamford Marriott dining room converted into a sort of exam room, tables set with dividers. Reminiscent of nervous SAT takers, a few hundred attendees sat with pencils ready while proctors distributed puzzles, facedown. When Will Shortz gave the word, everyone flipped his or her papers. As solvers finished a puzzle, hands shot up and proctors rushed to collect the puzzles, noting the time. After the judges scored every puzzle for accuracy and speed, everyone convened on Sunday to watch the three top contestants complete the final crossword. The contestants wore earplugs so as not to be distracted by the crowd. In recent years, new categories have been added to allow for winners in subcategories, such as by age and home state. Due to the publicity after the release of *Wordplay*, the tournament experienced a surge of interest; as of 2008, the event moved to Brooklyn, New York, to accommodate about 700 contestants.

■ ▪ ▬ ▪ ■

Kahn was skeptical that anyone could physically complete a crossword correctly in less than 5 minutes, which was his best time. He had read about the 1982 winner, Stan Newman—then a bond analyst for E. F. Hutton but now a professional puzzle constructor and editor—who had solved the daily *Times* puzzle on television in 2.24 minutes. (Fourteen years later, Newman beat his own record under Guinness Book conditions and completed the Monday puzzle in 2.14 minutes.) Scribbling the alphabet into a blank grid without even looking at the clues took Kahn more than 4 minutes! (This was a ploy employed by Sir Alec Guinness, who filled in the cryptic to impress onlookers who were ignorant of the fact that he was simply filling in the blanks with random letters while acting the part of a puzzle solver.)

In March 1987, as a journalist writing for *The New Yorker*, Kahn came up to Stamford to see these whiz kids with his own eyes. When the three finalists raced against each other at the front of the auditorium, Rosen, then a computer programmer from Buffalo, New York, finished under six minutes for his third consecutive win. Perennial runner-up, Ellen Ripstein, a coworker of Rosen's from Metropolitan Life Insurance (winner of the 2001 tournament), completed shy of nine minutes. The second runner-up needed a full thirteen minutes. Kahn felt vindicated.

When crosswords were young, puzzle solvers clamored for contests. The first one to attract newspaper coverage took place at the Hotel Roosevelt in midtown Manhattan in the first week of 1925 and was billed as the first Intercollegiate Cross Word Puzzle Tournament. Two students each from Yale, Harvard, Princeton, and City College participated. Each team was given one clue to solve per round. Poet Stephen Vincent Benet and schoolmate Jack Thomas won for **ELI** by getting the winning answer to the *puzzle clue:* "Slight convex curve in the shaft of a column" (**ENTASIS**). The graceful answer, **ENTASIS**, describes an architectural detail, prefix from the Greek for "to stretch" and closing on the English plural letter **ESS**. Sour grapes to the Harvard losers, the playwright Robert E. Sherwood and newspaperman Heywood Hale Broun. Too bad that **ELY** Jacques Kahn, Harvard 1937, always on the lookout for a public way to solve crosswords, was too young to compete.

Winning money for puzzle solving was a marketing formula that caught on during the Depression. Newspapers dangled thousands in cash prizes for mailing in correctly filled diagrams. The *Chicago Herald and Examiner* ran a series of thirty crosswords in 1932 constructed by my crossword mentor, Eugene Sheffer, based on the theme of the Declaration of Independence. With $5,000 in prizes on offer, thousands of readers participated. Eventually, the competitive spirit reached a pitch more characteristic of field sports. As desperate solvers ripped up dictionaries to thwart the competition in those pre-

Internet times, librarians locked up their reference books. The issue generated much editorial debate in the *Library Journal*, which considered lobbying puzzle constructors to use encyclopedias in order to prevent dictionary abuse. (In those days, clues conformed to *Webster's* definitions, so they were easier to look up.)

It looks like the library cartel put the kibosh on puzzle contests because the concept went into the deep freeze for forty years. With the world back at war, newspapers put their resources back into covering the news. Puzzle solvers continued to fill away without the promise of financial reward. Prize solving came back to life in 1978, far from the library stacks, in a bookstore outside Cleveland. Hemming-Hulburt Booksellers put up a $1,000 grand prize for a novel stunt: A crossword marathon. Runners had been participating in the New York Marathon for eight years by that point, so why not try an endurance test for puzzle people? For twenty-four hours, the bookstore offered its premises and references as contestants wrestled with "The World's Hardest Puzzle" by top puzzle constructor Jordan S. Lasher, a chemical engineer by day. In his college years, Lasher had submitted a puzzle to Margaret Farrar. She sent it back with a few editorial recommendations. By the time he got around to resubmitting it to the *New York Times*, Will Weng bought it.

Of the 186 puzzle solvers brave enough to take the

Hemming-Hulburt challenge, Michael Donner, the first editor of *Games* magazine, took top honors. He completed Lasher's crossword after twenty-three hours of valiant solving, earning about $44 per hour for his trouble. The following year, the second editor of *Games*, the inimitable Will Shortz, took the prize money. Soon afterward, to the great benefit of the solving public, Shortz retired his racing pencil and became the voice of puzzles that has charmed, recruited, and engaged the new generation of puzzle solvers.

For puzzle solvers eager to go pro, keep your day job: Rather than cash, prizes in this industry tend to take the form of unabridged dictionaries. Imagine if *puzzle clue:* "Golfer Ernie" (**ELS**), the South African athlete, accepted payment in **TEES** (*puzzle clue:* "Starting places on the green")! The $5,000 **POT** for puzzle winnings set during the Depression by the *Chicago Herald and Examiner* with its Liberty Crossword Puzzle challenge seems frozen in time. The television show *Merv Griffin's Crosswords* offers five puzzle solvers the chance to speed solve on a projected grid, with the winner taking all. Creator of *Wheel of Fortune* and *Jeopardy*, the most popular game shows on television, Griffin was a lifelong acrossionado. He devised a multi-round TV game that would have warmed Kahn's solving soul. Round 1: Two puzzle solvers race to fill in a grid correctly. Round 2: Three additional solvers are added, and the stakes are doubled. Round 3: The player who has won the most money moves into the last solo round with the challenge of finishing the grid in ninety seconds on camera. Now that's pressure!

Speed solvers train, as do all athletes. Like a serious marathon runner, the speed solver competes against past performance and derives satisfaction by rubbing elbows with the **VIPS**. Participating is not simply about going for the **GOLD**: The goal is to finish the race. For best results, the speed solver concentrates on a single area of the crossword at a time, building on the first answer with confidence and answering as many of the nearby clues as possible. A scattershot approach does not make for optimal strategy. Think of the process like knitting, and stitch the words together, rather than rushing to the far side of the grid. If you think an answer is wrong, remove it, even if later you discover it turns out to be right. Some erasing is a necessary part of the game.

A puzzle a day at a minimum is the place to start. Additional recommendations from weaver Rebecca Kornbluh—1984–1986 winner of the short-lived *Games* magazine U.S. Open—are to skim the news for current four-letter names, and to devote more time to playing Scrabble. While Scrabble does not allow proper nouns or foreign words, it helps train your eye to create words out of a jumble of letters. My personal favorite version of the game, Speed Scrabble, is played with tiles only. Each player selects seven tiles. At the call to start, each player turns over his or her tiles. Using these letters, the player creates an individual grid of six letters, with two or possibly three intersecting words, selecting one letter to pass along. The first player to finish calls out the word *switch*, passes the rejected tile to the player at the right, and turns over two tiles from the general pile. Each player then incorporates the new tiles into his or her grid, always rejecting one to pass along at the word *switch*. Obvious rejects are *Q* and *Z*, which usually get passed around. The game is played until the tiles are depleted and one person calls out the word *finished*. If no one has any questions about the winner's grid, the points on the tiles are added up. Losers deduct the number of points of the unused letters. Each round takes fifteen or twenty minutes max, a great change from the long, tedious hours of Scrabble when your opponent is angling for double and triple word scores. Lose the grid and try this new spin for those with limited attention spans.

Speed-solving crossword pros agree on three exercises for the **TYRO** contestant:

- *If an answer stumps you, look it up.* Take advantage of references. Rely on your computer for the answer to every sticky clue at your fingertips. Adding new words, especially of the four-letter variety, is one of the big rewards for spending this much time hanging out with crosswords. Chances are the word will repeat in a future grid, and you will have the answer ready to go.

- *Time yourself when solving on your own.* Get an idea of how much time you need per puzzle. If you scan the clues for missing links and work your way through to tricky clues, you will move more quickly.

- *Improve hand–eye coordination.* Like a **STENO** in the courtroom, you must scribble quickly! Your handwriting may be slowing you down, which means you should streamline your upper-case letters. For example, convert a **C** into an **E** with the flick of a dash, which shaves one second off composing the letter properly. With the dominance of **E** in this game, imagine how your solving time will improve thanks to this little trick.

Hinman, youngest puzzle winner in Stamford history, adds this helpful tidbit: If stuck, stare. He explains that if you look long enough, you might recognize familiar letter patterns even without reading the clue. For example, *puzzle clue:* "Ship launched from Iolcus." Greek ship, four letters? If you saw **A – G –**, how would you complete the word? Up pops the mythical **ARGO**, the frigate that carried Jason and crew to the Black Sea in their search for the Golden Fleece. Now a tiny village on the coast of Thessaly, thirteenth-century BCE, Iolcus drew immortals such as **HERA** (*puzzle clue:* "Wife of Zeus"). Besides the name of his ship, Jason leaves crosswords his bereaved wife, immortalized by Euripides, the five-letter repeater **MEDEA**. His granny, **TYRO**, offers an obscure alternative to the Latin definition of the word that I have used more than once in these pages (*puzzle clue:* "Beginner").

In the interest of time, Hinman has trained himself to write one answer while reading the next clue. The world's fastest speed solver, Stan Newman, Stamford 1982, now editor of the syndicated *Newsday* crossword, reveals that one of his secret weapons was creating a deck of crossword flash cards. In the 1980s, pre–personal computer days, Stan filled boxes with index cards of handwritten keywords. Scribbling the words in your handwriting helps with retention.

At the other end of the spectrum, Stamford winner Rosen compares prepping for a crossword competition to studying for an IQ test. He does concede, however, that trying your hand at crossword construction can yield insights into what makes a crossword tick. Puzzle master Shortz observes that well-rounded generalists make competent solvers because they have a smattering of knowledge on many subjects.

And finally, the high-IQ-society Mensa offers this formula for any test taker:

Skip over what you don't know.

Review your answers.

Hazard a guess where necessary.

Get a good night's sleep.

Sufficient shut-eye adds 10 percent to the final outcome: In the final analysis, a restful night is the only guarantee for improving your puzzle performance.

13

THE FUTURE OF FOUR-LETTER WORDS:
"The — the Limit"

I do the New York Times crossword every day. You have to understand, it's how I comb my brain every morning.

NORMAN MAILER, PULITZER PRIZE–WINNING
AUTHOR AND PUZZLE SOLVER

On the occasion of his eightieth birthday, in an interview for *Newsweek* magazine, the late Norman Mailer, two-time Pulitzer winner, described his puzzle habit as a way of keeping his brain slicked back. Mailer, of course, chronicled his World War II service in *The Naked and the Dead*, hailed as one of the greatest books of the twentieth century. Despite the **KUDOS**, the writer's secret aspiration was to be a crossword repeater. His is a vowel-rich surname, yet the fact that he was not a repeater rubbed him the wrong way. From a lifetime of crossword solving, Mailer recognized the puzzle power of vowels, as illustrated by words we have explored in these pages. Experts have analyzed that vowels fill half a typical grid, whereas on an average printed page, like this one, consonants dominate. Vowels connect Across with Down. But Mailer did not take into account the length of his name: Those two additional letters put him forever in the shadow of his contemporary, **URIS** (*puzzle clue:* "Author Leon"). Bestselling author of *Exodus*, *Trinity*, and **MILA** ("— 18"), Uris recounted his Marine days during World War II in his bestselling *Battle Cry.* A four-letter surname that alternates vowel with consonant and ends with an **S** guarantees immortality in crossword puzzles. By this measure, repeaterdom is in the cards for *puzzle clue:* "Author Martin" (**AMIS**), author of *London Fields.*

Since Christmas 1913 when the crossword made its debut, four-letter words have proven their mettle. Even in the early days, the issue was divisive: Fans find the little words educational, while critics deplore the constant recycling. In defense of four-letter words, a 1925 essay in *The Literary Digest* (later merged into *Time* magazine) applauded the crossword for reintroducing useful ones into daily speech. Could it be a coincidence that the essayist Arthur Bartlett Maurice was a colleague of John Farrar, consort of crossword's First Lady? Specifically, Maurice welcomed back **ABET** and **EMIT**. Not exactly e-mail user's terms, these two words illustrate the ideal crossword vowel-consonant sequence. *Puzzle clue:* "Support a felon" (**ABET**) comes from the old French "to entice" and lives on as half of the courtroom phrase "aid and abet," thanks to TV shows like *Law and Order*. It is removed by one vowel from real estate repeater **ABUT** (*puzzle clue:* "Border on"). **EMIT**, of Shakespearean vintage, answers to the synonym *puzzle clue:* "Radiate" or the less obvious *puzzle clue:* "Give out." Change the first consonant to yield **EDIT**, or the first vowel for **OMIT**, both habitués of the grid.

Maurice cheered the reappearance of a select group of three-letter words—**ERR**, **IRE**, and **NEE**—all of which continue to suffer from grid overexposure. Each connects to *puzzle clues:* "Go off," "Anger," and "Society page word," respectively. Maurice also gave puzzles credit for dusting off two parts of a cathedral—namely **APSE** and **NAVE**. Still going strong, *puzzle clue:* "Place for a fresco, maybe" (from the Greek word for "arch"), the **APSE** is the domed part of the church that houses the altar. Due to its awkward third letter, puzzle solvers see less of **NAVE**, the central aisle that leads to the **APSE**. In architectural terms, it descends from the **STOA** (*puzzle clue:* "Greek portico," a clue that is in semiretirement). The covered walkway familiar to Sophocles has gone the way of the **AGORA** (*puzzle clue:* "Ancient Greek marketplace"). Ancestor of today's four-letter **MALL**, the five-letter repeater is composed of more congenial crossword components.

Refuting Maurice's positive spin, the *New York Times* belittled four-letter words in an editorial. "Egypt made her place in history secure by developing a bird named **IBIS** and a goddess named **ISIS**.... There is only one world language worth speaking of. It is **ERSE**." This is the point made by Franklin Pierce Adams—newspaperman and Algonquin Round Table wit (and Margaret Farrar's unofficial proofreader)—in his spoof "Vocabulary Enrichment in the Suburbs Due to the Crossword Puzzle Influence":

MRS. F: Are you making that **EBON** garment for yourself?

MRS. W: **YEA**. Henry says I look rather **NAIF** in black.

MRS. F: Well perhaps but it's a bit too **ANILE** for me. Give me something in indigo or say **ECRU**.

Beige to the discerning eye turns to **ECRU**, a grayish yellow, in puzzledom. Puzzle solvers know the difference.

With stale four-letter words being put out to pasture, the puzzle solver justifiably wonders if the lexicon is contracting. Or, can it be long before puzzle constructors weave in four-letter words that answer to the Henry Hook *puzzle clue:* "Four-letter word, aptly" (**OATH**)? True, in our lifetime, four-letter words once disguised by quaint euphemisms like "H, E, double hockey sticks" have worked their way into the main-stream media. Yes, puzzle constructors favor **S** words. However, even with the passage of four-score-plus years, crossword puzzle constructors continue to follow Farrar's original dictum: Good news preferred. If faced with **SHI** – to complete the four-letter word, the puzzle constructor can choose from among multiple G-rated consonants or even the vowels **A** and **I**, *puzzle clues:* "Muslim sect" and "Member of Muslim sect." Problem solved.

Rather than alienate the audience, crossword puzzle publishers compile a list of verboten words that are banished to **ELBA** (*puzzle clue:* "Isle of exile"). The only four-letter expletives encountered by the present-day puzzle solver qualify as *puzzle clue:* "Cry from Charlie Brown" (**DRAT**, **DARN**, or **RATS**). A term like **SCUM**, in the sense of soapy film, occasionally makes a cameo appearance. Answer to the innocuous *puzzle clue:* "Polish leader Walesa" does occasionally present as "Lustful one, informally" (**LECH**, short for *lecher*). Yes, slang is acceptable, not unpleasantness.

Slang supplies standbys like **GAGA**, in the sense of "crazy" or "infatuated," and **BLAH**, first syllable of blasé as in "boring." From Gaelic, or the confounded **ERSE**, puzzle constructors borrow **GLOM** (*puzzle clue:* "Latch (onto)"). Hip-hop music has contributed **PHAT** (*puzzle clue:* "Excellent, slangily"). The negative connotations of fat are reversed by this alternate spelling. It belongs to the lexicon generated by the film **BOYZ** *n the Hood*, which carries the burden of a final **Z**. In the three-letter category, hip-hop has produced a solid repeater with **DIS** (*puzzle clue:* "Slam"). Simply the first syllable of *disrespect*, it provides a fresh clue for the negative prefix and has become a commonly used term in conversation.

Any slang word that enters the mainstream is a candidate, thanks to Will Shortz, who believes that crosswords need to reflect real life. Borrowing from the drug culture is included, as in the newly minted repeater **ODED** (*puzzle clue:* "Did too much, in a way"). The initials for *over* and *dosed*, the verb now applies to doing too much of anything—from coffee drinking to TV viewing. It is one letter removed from the omnipresent three-part lyric poems penned by John Keats or Pindar, **ODES**, originally accompanied by the harp's progenitor, or **LYRE**. Other shorthand phrases from the era of e-mail communication include **OKOK** (*puzzle clue:* "All right, already"). It might answer the nagging call **CMON** (*puzzle clue:* "Follow me!"), the elision for "come on."

━ ▭ ━

For the past ten years, NPR's puzzle master Shortz has sanctioned a formerly untapped source of four-letter words for use in crosswords: Trade names. Rather than the tired missing-link *puzzle clue:* "Rara —" for **AVIS**, the clue has become "Hertz rival." Encountering a car rental company is more amusing for the puzzle solver than the Latin phrase for rare bird or unique person, in Crosswordese known also as an **ONER**. Through osmosis, puzzle solvers are experts on a wide variety of brands. General knowledge helps in navigating today's grid, which puts more distance between the modern pastime and the dictionary exercise.

E leads the way in crossword repeaters with **ESSO** and **EGGO**. Although Standard Oil (S.O., pronounced **ESSO** and *puzzle clue:* "Bygone US gas brand") officially adopted the double **X** five-letter name Exxon, its original name is a puzzle perennial. Because drivers still pump **ESSO** overseas, it continues as *puzzle clue:* "Gas brand in Canada" or "Petrol seller" (the British vernacular for *petroleum*). Although few puzzle solvers recall the **ESSO** slogan ("Put a tiger in your tank"), many have heard the memorable slogan, "L'eggo my **EGGO**." Once the frozen waffle maker **EGGO** diversified into French toast sticks and other breakfast specialties, it offered more clue options. This is the sort of development that warms the fingers of crossword constructors. The four-letter snack of choice in America is the top-selling cookie **OREO** (*puzzle clue:* "Crème-filled snack"). Ice cream makers added it as a flavor, which creates a second dimension to its repertoire.

Puzzle pets choose between **ALPO** (*puzzle clue:* "Bowlful for Spot") and **IAMS** (*puzzle clue:* "Good for life sloganeer").

When not chugging **ALE**, the puzzle solver favors **NEHI**, disguised as *puzzle clue:* "Old pop," in the sense of lowercase soda pop rather than dear old Dad. Pronounced *knee high*, the soft drink was named for an advertising campaign that dates to the crossword's youth, which combined a stocking and a female knee. Sales peaked during World War II, yet **NEHI** lives on in reruns thanks to the TV series **MASH** and the drinking habits of a character called Radar. The solver who ODs on **OREOS** and **NEHI** can reach for *puzzle clue:* "— Seltzer" (**ALKA**).

Trade names fill the shelves of the baby boomer's medicine cabinet, as well as the squares in the crossword grid, such as: "Oil of —" (**OLAY**), "Hair-removal option" (**NAIR**), and "Pfizer product used before brushing teeth" (**PLAX**). Is there a solver among us who does not recognize **QTIP** as the answer to *puzzle clue:* "Cosmetics applicator" or, repulsively, "Wax remover?" You may even find the modern cure-all brand name **ADVIL**. For bathroom fixtures, the puzzle solver covets *puzzle clue:* "Big name in faucets" for **MOEN**, which rhymes with **COEN** (*puzzle clue:* "Joel and Ethan of film"). Charge all household items to **VISA** (*puzzle clue:* "MasterCard rival") or **AMEX** (*puzzle clue:* "Visa alternative, for short").

Parked in the puzzle garage is either an **OPEL** (*puzzle clue:* "European auto"), surname of the Henry Ford of Germany, or **AUDI** (*puzzle clue:* "German auto"), acronym for Auto Union

Deutschland Ingolstadt. In the corner of the garage, there lurks a **TORO** (*puzzle clue:* "Lawn-mower handle," in which *handle* means "nickname"). Zoom off to **IHOP** (*puzzle clue:* "Restaurant acronym") before a stop at another familiar acronym, **IKEA** (*puzzle clue:* "Swedish-based chain"). In 1943 Ingvar Kamprad tacked his initials **IK** onto those of his childhood farm Elmtaryd and his village of Agunnaryd to create a vowel-rich four-letter brand. Four decades later, the store opened an outlet in the United States, which became a mainstay in American housewares as well as a popular puzzle repeater. Next door, Denmark contributes **LEGO** (*puzzle clue:* "Brand of blocks"). This repeater is an abbreviated version of the Danish phrase *leg godt*, which translates as "play well." That is a motto with which puzzle solvers can agree.

■□□□

With Shortz's blessing, puzzle constructors scout pop culture for four-letter words. Awards, from **CLIO** (advertising) to **EMMY** (television), **OBIE** (dramatists), and **TONY** (stage), are mainstays. Classic rock groups like the British "Jethro —" (**TULL**) enjoy steady grid exposure. Of *Aqualung* fame, circa 1971, the musical group eclipses Jethro Tull, inventor of the seed drill (in 1701). Although Tull was responsible for improving crop yield on a worldwide basis and feeding the masses for centuries, his name remains in the public consciousness mostly because a booking agent randomly chose it for a band of six musicians forty years ago. Heavy-metal 1970s Australian group **ACDC** (*puzzle clue:* "'Back in Black' rock band") is catching on. Puzzle constructors are grateful for a musical twist to the dictionary definition for alternating current and direct current. Australia also gave us **INXS** (*puzzle clue:* "'Suicide Blonde' band"), which offers the otherwise impossible juxtaposition of **X** with **S**. How lucky for puzzle constructors that the members of the band chose to spell *in excess* with four letters.

▄ ▄ ▄ ▄

The Space Age delivered one sturdy four-letter repeater in **NASA**; in the three-letter category, the space craft **LEM** (for lunar excursion module) and the space station **MIR** appear as often as **UFO**. But of all techie developments, none matches the potential for four-letter words that computers promise. The Internet has unleashed a torrent of four-letter terms, some with hopes of becoming repeaters. Unlikely consonant sequences **HTTP** (hypertext transfer protocol), **HTML** (hypertext markup language), and **DSL** (digital subscriber line) spice up the old crop of repeaters. Even with its awkward initial **J** and final **G**, puzzle constructors throw in the occasional **JPEG** (joint photographic experts group), the standard for *puzzle clue:* "Computer graphics file," which compresses and decompresses images for display on screen. A likelier candidate is *puzzle clue:* "Modern journal" (**BLOG**, the contraction of the words *web log*). None of these newly minted four-letter words shows the stamina of **WIFI**, the wireless neologism with its winning consonant-vowel configuration. A term bequeathed by laptop culture, it answers to *puzzle clue:* "Kind of computer connection" or "Modern kind of network." Even **SPAM** gets a makeover thanks to **EMAIL**. No longer just the tinned meat product of the Monty Python song, it means unsolicited e-mail and goes by *puzzle clue:* "Some term life offers."

Apple has guaranteed its role in crosswords with its Macintosh brand. Crossword constructors playfully clue **IMAC**, a desktop computer, as *puzzle clue:* "Apple product" and "Apple on teacher's desk?" The portable four-letter word **IPOD** (*puzzle clue:* "Song holder") comes in two puzzle-friendly models: **NANO** and **MINI**. At last, the skirt style goes on hiatus. The midi length never caught on, despite its secondary French-language *puzzle clue:* "Noon, in Nantes."

The boob tube plays a serious role in crosswords, more so since the advent of cable options with puzzle-friendly call letters like **HBO** and **ESPN** (*puzzle clue:* "NASCAR airer"). TV sitcoms provide grid fodder, starting with the 1950s **DESI** from the classic *I Love Lucy*, aired on Nick at **NITE** (on the Nickelodeon channel). The following decade contributes

MRED (*Mister Ed*), the talking palomino of prime time. Based on the book by children's author Walter R. Brooks, it's a show about the relationship between a talking horse and his owner, Wilbur Post. From the same era, puzzle solvers recognize Academy Award–winning director Ron Howard (*A Beautiful Mind*), frozen in time as **OPIE** (*puzzle clue:* "Mayberry boy"), the six-year-old from *The Andy Griffith Show.*

If puzzle constructors named one show for most puzzle material, however, it would be the 1990s animated series *The Simpsons.* Populated by characters with puzzle-friendly names, it offers new clues for old stand-bys **LISA**, bartender **MOE**, and schoolteacher **EDNA** Krabappel. Mrs. K has overtaken twentieth-century writers Ferber and St. Vincent Millay. Video technology has developed the **TIVO** recording device to time-shift programs for *après* crosswords, or whenever the mood strikes. What an improvement over the **VCR**, the infernal video cassette recorder of the 1980s—a vowel-deficient item that was never ready for puzzle prime time.

———

Thirty years ago, Eugene T. Maleska fretted that puzzle constructors were a dying breed, but his fears were unfounded. As it turns out, the industry requires only a few hundred creative spirits and their computers to keep one in ten Americans entertained. The *New York Times* counts just 110 different crossword bylines per year. Of these, many are hobbyists rather than pro-fessionals. Putting together a crossword is a labor of love. A conventional crossword takes half a day or so to construct, even with computer technology, but maybe an hour or less to solve. The aim is to provide amusement, to allow the puzzle solver that **AHA** (*puzzle clue:* "Eureka") moment, not to stump or humiliate. Getting the answers to clues provides a workout for the mind as beneficial to the brain cells as pumping iron is to the muscles.

When I started out in the crossword field, all and sundry would remark to me, "My mother loves puzzles." Everyone's mother still turns to the puzzle page, but the demographic is no longer skewed to females. Now it includes members of **AARP** (*puzzle clue:* "Modern Maturity org.") as well as an influx of **GENX** solvers, thanks to the cool attitude introduced by Will Shortz. It is becoming harder to resist the visceral attraction of a black-and-white grid. In the words of longtime puzzle solver and award-winning author Russell Baker: "Show me a blank grid and I want to fill it." That's how many of us feel—drawn to the challenge of empty boxes, fresh clues, and a stockpile of reliable and potent four-letter words.

Appendix

Reproduced here is the mimeographed guideline sheet that Eugene T. Maleska mailed to me in 1978 in reply to my original query, which has been in my files ever since:

The New York Times, New York, N.Y. 10036

Daily puzzles – 15 × 15 squares with over-all balanced pattern of black squares. Keep word total at 76 or under, with a minimum word length of three letters. Puzzles with 78 entries will be considered if they have a theme.

SUNDAY – 23 × 23 and 21 × 21, with a word total of 170 or under for 23's and 140 or under for 21's. Also diagramless puzzles of unusual shapes and sizes up to 23 squares, but word count must be kept between 82 and 86. Minimum word length of three letters on all puzzles.

Two patterns on separate typewriter-sized sheets, with squares measuring a bit over ¼ inch. One pattern containing numbers only, for test solving, and the other containing <u>both</u> numbers and words. Make the black square plainly visible.

Name and address (with zip code and Social Security number) on both diagrams and on first page of definitions. List definitions double-spaced on typewriter sized paper. Definitions at left and answers at far right, with no periods after either numbers of definitions. The Down words need not start on a new page. Sample of defs:

ACROSS

1	Dashing young man	blade
6	Lion's —	share
11	Largest lake in Europe	Ladoga (Lipp Gaz)
24	Army officer: Abbr.	Brig. Gen (Web. Coll)

Stamped, addressed return envelope with every puzzle. Puzzles may be folded for mailing. Use paper clips rather than staples.

Except for informal words or phrases, all words or abbreviations must come from a standard reference source.

For the large puzzles particularly, some kind of underlying theme is preferred for the longer entries. Many of the inner-clue topics, such as flowers, cities, articles of clothing, have been overworked but there are always new approaches and variations available. The concerns and foibles of life are almost always good puzzle fodder. Phrases are fine if they reasonably familiar or logical, but avoid awkward or artificial ones such as "was in session" or "greet friends." Go easy on proper names, especially first names that can be defined only as "Girl's name," or names of people who are in the news now but who may be all but forgotten in a matter of months. Also avoid trade names and strained "re" words ("rehesitate," "redrown"). In the shorter words especially, see if the rarer letters can be used to get away from a parade of s, r, e and t words. Keep foreign, obsolete and variant words to a minimum, but if one is used make sure it does not make a blind crossing with another obscure word. Avoid combinations with "a" ("a hotel," "deliver a") unless they can be defined as part of a legitimate phrase.

For the daily puzzles, look for words and phrases that you think the solver might find interesting. Words such as "assessment" or "re-investigations" are not likely to provide much of a lift.

Essential Crosswordese

A

AARE.........................Swiss river

AARP.........................Modern Maturity org.

ABBA.........................Swedish rock group

ABE.........................Justice Fortas

ABED.........................Retired

ABET.........................Support, as a felon

ABLE........................."— was I ere I saw…"

ABUT.........................Border (upon)

ACDC........................."Back in Black" band

ACE.........................Master

Top notch

ADAR.........................Hebrew month

ADE.........................Summer cooler

ADO.........................Fuss

AERIE .... Penthouse

AERO .... Space opener

AGEE .... Author James

AGORA .... Greek marketplace

AGRI .... Cultural beginning?

AHA .... Eureka!

AIRE .... River of Leeds

ALA .... — carte

ALAI .... Jai —

ALAN .... Actor Alda

ALAR .... Banned apple spray

ALAS .... "—, poor Yorick…"

                             Expression of woe

ALDA .... Hawkeye portrayer

ALE .... Pub order

ALEC .... Actor Baldwin

ALEE .... To shelter, nautically

ALKA .... — Seltzer

ALLO .... French greeting

ALOE .... — vera

ALOT .... Thanks —!

ALOU .... Baseball family name

ALPO .... Bowlful for Spot

ALTO .... Choir member

ALVA............................Part of TAE
AMA ....MD's org.
AMAH ....Asian governess
AMAT ....Latin I verb
                         Amo, amas, —
AMI............................Boyfriend, in Brest
AMIN ....Subject of "The Last King of Scotland"
ANAT ....Med school subject
ANILE.......................Old womanish
ANKA........................"Puppy Love" singer Paul
ANNA........................"— Karenina"
ANNO........................Part of A.D.
APE.............................Copy
APER..........................Copycat
APET..........................In — (peeved)
APOP ....Each
APPT ....Diary abbr.
ARAL..........................Landlocked sea
ARAN........................Galway Bay islands
ARGO ....Jason's ship
ARIL...........................Seed cover
ARLO..........................A Guthrie
ARON ....Elvis — Presley
ASIS............................Words on a sales tag

ASTA........................ "Thin Man" pooch
ATE........................... Chowed down
ATON........................ Massive amount
ATSEA....................... Confused
ATTAR...................... Perfume essence
ATTU........................ Aleutian island
AUDI......................... German car
AULD........................ "— Lang Syne"
AVA........................... Actress Gardner
AVE........................... Latin greeting
AVIS......................... Hertz rival
AVON........................ Bard's river

B

BAIT........................ Lure
BARA........................ Silent film star Theda
BELA........................ Actor Lugosi
BETA........................ Phi — Kappa
BLAH........................ Nondescript
BLOG........................ Modern journal
BOCA........................ — Raton

C

CASA .... Hombre's home
                           Latin quarters?
CHAI .... Starbucks option
CIAO .... Farewell, in Florence
CLIO .... Advertising award
CMON .... Let's go!
COEN .... Film director Joel

D

DADA .... WWI art movement
DAHL .... Author Roald
DALI .... Spanish surrealist Salvador
DARN .... Mild expletive
DDAY .... WWII turning point
                           June 6, 1944
DELE .... Remove from a text
DEMI .... G.I. Jane portrayer
DIS .... Slam
DOH .... Homer's head-slapping remark
DORA .... "— the Explorer"

DRAT.........................Mild oath
DREI.........................German crowd?

E

EBAN.........................Statesman Abba
EBAY.........................Silent auction site
ECON.........................MBA subject
ECRU.........................Nude shade
ECTO.........................Prefix with morph
EDEN.........................Land of temptation
                       Prime Minister Anthony
EDER.........................River of Hesse
EDIE.........................Actress Falco
EDIT.........................Red pencil, e.g.
EDNA.........................Mrs. Krabappel
EDO.........................Tokyo, once
EEE.........................Wide foot spec
EERO.........................Architect Saarinen
EGAL.........................Equal, in Evian
EGAD.........................Mild oath
EGAN.........................Richard of old Westerns
EGGO.........................Waffle maker
EKE.........................Scrape by, with "out"
ELAL.........................Mideast airline

ELAN......................Flair
ELBA......................Isle of exile
ELEE......................Gen. Robt. —
ELI.........................Yalie
ELIA......................Director Kazan
ELIE......................Author Wiesel
ELLA......................First lady of song
ELLE......................Supermodel Macpherson
ELLO......................Cockney greeting
ELS........................Golfer Ernie
ELSE......................Or —!
ELUL......................Hebrew month
EMIT......................Radiate
EMMA...................Jane Austen heroine
EMMY...................TV award
ENDO....................Prefix with skeleton
ENID.....................Author Bagnold
EPEE.....................Three-sided blade
                    Dueling sword
ERA......................Important time
ERAT....................Part of Q.E.D.
ERIE.....................Great lake
ERLE.....................First name in mystery
ERMA...................Witty Bombeck
                    Author Bombeck

ERNE........................ Sea eagle

Coastal flier

EROS........................ Hermes' son

ERR........................... Stray

ERS .... Bitter vetch

ERSE .... Gaelic

ERST........................ Once, once

ERTE........................ Deco designer

ESAI .... Morales of "NYPD Blue"

ESNE........................ Anglo-Saxon slave

ESPN........................ NASCAR airer

ESSE........................ To be, to Brutus

ESSO .... Petrol seller

ESTE .... Villa d'—

ETA........................... Airport letters

ETAL........................ List ender

ETAT........................ Coup d'—

ETC........................... List ender

ETE........................... Nice season

ETRE........................ Raison d'—

ETTE........................ Major finale?

ETUI .... Decorative case

EURO....................... Continental coin

EVA........................... Actress Longoria

EVER .... Hardly —

F

FALA..........................FDR's pet

G

GAGA........................Smitten
GALA........................Senora Dali
GENX........................Baby boomers' babies
GERE........................Dr. T portrayer
GLOM........................Latch (onto)
GRAF........................Five-time US Open champ

H

HARI........................Mata —
HAUS........................Hamburger's home
HEHE........................Giggle
HERA........................Wife of Zeus
HOLM........................Actress Celeste
HULA........................— hoop

I

IAMS .... "Good for Life" sloganeer
IBIS .... Wading bird
ICAN .... Volunteer's phrase
IDEE .... Brainstorm in Paris
IDO .... Wedding vow
IGOR .... Composer Stravinsky
IHOP .... Restaurant acronym
IKEA .... Swedish-based chain
ILIE .... Nastase of tennis
IMUS .... Shock jock Don
INGA .... Swenson of Benson
INGE .... "Picnic" playwright
INXS .... "Suicide Blonde" band
IOTA .... Jot
IOU .... Red-ink letters
IPOD .... Song holder
IRA .... Retirement fund letters
IRAE .... Dies —
IRE .... Anger
ISEE .... Understanding phrase
ISIS .... Egyptian goddess
ISLA .... Ibiza, e.g.

ISLE............................Capri, e.g.
ITER............................Brain passage

K

KUDOS......................High praise
                        Accolades

L

LAIT............................Café au —
LATTE.......................Tall coffee order
LAYS...........................Potato chip maker
LECH.........................Polish leader Walesa
LEGO.........................Brand of blocks
LEI..............................Hawaiian neckwear
LENA.........................Siberian river
LENO.........................Carson successor
LIEU...........................Stead
LIRA...........................Old Italian bread
LITE............................Low-cal
LOO............................W.C.

LOOS .... Writer Anita
LUAU .... Hawaiian cookout

M

MASH .... Hawkeye show
MATT .... Actor Damon
MAYA .... Poet Angelou
MEDEA .... Euripides tragic heroine
MEGA .... Large: prefix
MIA .... Actress Farrow
MIES .... Architect — van der Rohe
MILA .... "— 18"
MINI .... Certain iPod
MOEN .... Big name in faucets
MONT .... — Blanc
MRED .... Wilbur Post's friend

N

NAIR .... Hair-removal option
NANA .... Peter Pan pet
NAPA .... Sonoma County neighbor

NAVE..........................Cathedral aisle
NAZI..........................Extra in "The Producers"
NEAL..........................Actress Patricia
NEAP..........................Type of tide
NEE..........................Society page word
NEHI..........................Old pop
NENE..........................Hawaiian goose
NERD..........................Egghead sort
NEVA..........................Russian river
NINA..........................One of a sailboat trio
NOEL..........................Carol
NOIR..........................Film —
NORA..........................Author Ephron
NORAH..................Singer Jones
NYSE..........................Wall Street inst.

O

OAHU..........................Waikiki locale
OATH..........................Four-letter word, aptly
OBI..........................Kimono sash
OBIE..........................Broadway award
ODE..........................Keatsian form
ODEA..........................Old music halls

ODED .... Did too much, in a way
ODES .... Pindar output
OGEE........................ Curved molding
OKOK .... All right, already!
OLAV .... Patron saint of Norway
OLAY .... Oil of —
OLE............................ Corrida cheer
OLIO.......................... Hodgepodge
OLLA .... Earthenware jug
OMAN....................... Sultanate
OMAR....................... Actor Epps
OMIT......................... Leave out
ONER........................ Unique person
OONA........................ Mrs. Chaplin
OPEL......................... European auto
OPIE.......................... "Mayberry" boy
ORAN........................ Camus' birthplace
ORCA........................ Killer whale
OREM........................ City east of Utah Lake
OREO........................ Crème-filled snack
ORLY......................... Paris hub
ORT .... Morsel
OSHA........................ Fed watchdog
OSTE........................ Bone: prefix
OTT........................... Baseball name of fame

OUSE .... River of NE England
OVEN .... Pizzeria fixture

P

PAAR .... Carson predecessor
PEDI .... Cure opener
PESO .... Mexican money
PHAT .... Excellent, slangily
PLAX .... Mouthwash
POOH .... Winnie-the- —

Q

QTIP .... Wax remover?

R

RAH .... Cheer
RAND .... Author Ayn
RANI .... Hindu princess
RATA .... Pro —

RATS.........................Cry from Charlie Brown
RAVI ....Sitarist Shankar
RILL ....Streamlet
RONA.........................Author Jaffe
ROSH ....— Hashanah
RYAN.........................Actor O'Neal

S

SAKE ....Drink with sushi
SANS.........................Without
SASE ....Ms. enclosure
SCAT.........................Beat it!
SEER ....Clairvoyant
SERE ....Like the Sahara
SHEA.........................Queens stadium
SHEL.........................Author Silverstein
SHOO.........................Beat it!
SISI.............................Spanish words of encouragement
SNAP ....Cinch
SOS ....Help!
SOSA.........................Sammy of baseball
SOSO.........................Middling

SRA.............................Madrid Mrs.

SRO.............................Sellout letters

SSN.............................Personal data: Abbr.

STE.............................Sault — Marie

STER...........................Poll closing?

STLO...........................WWII battle site

Capital of La Manche

STOA...........................Greek portico

T

TACO...........................South of the border order

TALI............................Ankle bones

TARA...........................Scarlett's home

TARO...........................Poi source

TATE...........................Gallery showing Turner

TEES...........................Starting places on the green

TELE...........................Distance: prefix

TERI............................Actress Hatcher

TESS...........................— of the d'Urbervilles

TETE...........................French thinker?

THEO..........................Huxtable son

TIVO...........................Recording device

TONY..........................Stage award
TORO..........................Corrida creature
                            Lawn-mower handle
TOTO..........................Dorothy's dog
TSAR..........................Ivan, for one
TULL..........................Jethro —
TYRO..........................Beginner

U

UCLA..........................Campus NW of LA
ULAN..........................— Bator
URAL..........................Russian mountain range
URIS..........................Author Leon
USAF..........................B-52 org.
USDA..........................Letters before prime
USSR..........................WWII ally

V

VIDI..........................Veni, —, vici
VISA..........................MasterCard rival
VOLE..........................Mouselike rodent

W

WIFI...........................Kind of computer connection
WISE...........................Director Robert

Y

YEAH ....Slangy assent
YSER ....Belgian river

Z

ZASU ....Silent film star Pitts

Bibliography

Articles

Arnot, Michelle, *Herald Tribune Crosswords,* series of interviews with celebrity puzzle solvers, 1984–1986:

"Mind-Jogging with James Fixx," June 1984

"From A to Laura Z. (Hobson)," July 1984

"Tuning in to Puzzles with Richard Maltby Jr.," August 1984

"A Chat with Chast: Cartoonist Roz Chast," September 1984

"Remembering Margaret Farrar," November 1984

"Beverly Sills, Prima Puzzler," January 1985

"Keith Hernandez: Grand Slam Puzzler," March 1985

"Russell Baker: Pulitzer Prize Puzzler," May 1985

"All About Puzzles: Celeste Holm," July 1985

"Dick Cavett: Man of Letters," August 1985

"Post Haste Puzzler: Ben Bradlee," October 1985

"A Learned Puzzler: Actress Michael Learned," November 1985

"Norman Cousins: The Power of Positive Puzzling," December 1985

"Thomas Middleton: Double-Crostician," March 1986

"1 Across: Roy Blount Jr.," April 1986

"Press Box Puzzler, E. J. Kahn Jr.," May 1986

"Rukeyser's Wall Street Weakness: Puzzles," December 1986

Balfour, Sandy, "A Great British Obsession," *The Guardian Weekend*, January 25, 2003.

Buranelli, Prosper, et al., "How the Crossword Craze Started, by the Starters," *Colliers*, January 31, 1925.

Farrar, Margaret, "Guest Word: A Puzzlement," *The New York Times*, April 7, 1974.

Folkedahl, Terry, "The Secret of Youth: Crosswords," *The Daily Herald*, Arlington Heights, IL, April 6, 1985.

Germain, David, "Crossword Guru Shortz," *Associated Press*, January 23, 2006.

"Hangin' with Matt Damon," AGirlsWorld.com, June 2002.

Kahn Jr., E. J., "Coble and Ten K," *The New Yorker*, May 11, 1987.

"Never a Cross Word," *Good Housekeeping*, June 1956.

Newman, Stan, "7 Steps to Better Solving," *American Federation of Crosswords*, Fall 1986.

Newsweek, "Norman Mailer Talks About Writing, Aging and Crossword Puzzles," January 19, 2003.

"Puzzle Plague," *Library Journal*, March 1, 1941.

Whipp, Glenn, "Crossword Mania Not Just for Squares," *Los Angeles Daily News*, June 18, 2006.

Books

Balfour, Sandy, *Pretty Girl in Crimson Rose (8)*, London: Tarcher, 2003.

Buranelli, Prosper, et al., *The Celebrity Cross Word Puzzle Book*, New York: Simon & Schuster, 1925.

Macnutt, D. S., *Ximenes on the Art of the Crossword Puzzle*, London: Methuen, 1966.

Toomey, Shamus, "Top Puzzler, 11 Letters," *Chicago Sun-Times*, April 6, 2007.

ACKNOWLEDGMENTS

Thank you to the following for their part in making this book:

Marian Lizzi, my editor at Perigee, for her guidance, encouragement, patience, and good judgment on *Four-Letter Words*. Rolph Blythe, agent and guardian angel of the proposal, for understanding the power of puzzles. Cornelia Read, mystery writer, for the introduction to Rolph. Alice Kaufman, writer and executive director of the Antique Tribal Art Dealers Association, with an acronym that has the hallmarks of a five-letter repeater, for the introduction to Cornelia. Nancy Gallt, children's book agent, for her enthusiastic encouragement in the early proposal phase. Alice van Straalen, editor, for asking if I had anything more to say about crosswords as we sipped wine at the New York Society Library annual awards party. Phyllis Schefer, art director, for bearing witness to the exchange with Alice van Straalen.

Thanks also to:

Will Shortz, NPR's Puzzle Master, for making crosswords cool, and to the many celebrity solvers for sharing their private passion with me. George Slowik, magazine publisher, for giving me free rein at *Herald*

Tribune Crosswords way back when. Many esteemed colleagues at Kappa Puzzle Group and *Games* magazine. Both my sisters: Jacqueline, for introducing me to Speed Scrabble, and Denise, for keeping the Scrabble games going.

And finally:

Hugo Arnot, the grandfather I never met, art supplier to Emperor Franz Josef, for passing along the puzzle gene. Roger Brown, my husband, who advised me to stop solving puzzles and construct one instead, and our daughter, Astrid, for teaching me how to speak Japanese.

ABOUT THE AUTHOR

Michelle Arnot is a writer and journalist who was pursuing a graduate degree in French eighteenth-century literature at Columbia University when she got sidetracked by crossword puzzles. She has served as editor and publisher of dozens of national puzzle magazines, most notably for the *Herald Tribune* and the Kappa Publishing Group. Author of two books about women's health and numerous books about puzzles, including *Crossword Puzzles for Dummies*, she is a native of New York City. Currently, she and her family spend most of the year in Tokyo.